The Cost of Raising Children in Canada

Robin A. Douthitt
and
Joanne Fedyk

Butterworths
Toronto and Vancouver

The Cost of Raising Children in Canada
© 1990 Butterworths Canada Ltd.

Printed and bound in Canada

The Butterworth Group of Companies

Canada:	Butterworths Canada Ltd., 75 Clegg Road, MARKHAM, Ontario, L6G 1A1 and 409 Granville St., Ste. 1455, VANCOUVER, B.C., V6C 1T2
Australia	Butterworths Pty Ltd., SYDNEY, MELBOURNE, BRISBANE, ADELAIDE, PERTH, CANBERRA and HOBART
Ireland	Butterworths (Ireland) Ltd., DUBLIN
New Zealand	Butterworths of New Zealand Ltd., WELLINGTON and AUCKLAND
Puerto Rico	Equity de Puerto Rico, Inc., HATO REY
Singapore	Malayan Law Journal Pte. Ltd., SINGAPORE
United Kingdom	Butterworth & Co. (Publishers) Ltd., LONDON and EDINBURGH
United States	Butterworth Legal Publishers, AUSTIN, Texas; BOSTON, Massachusetts; CLEARWATER, Florida (D & S Publishers); ORFORD, New Hampshire (Equity Publishing); ST. PAUL, Minnesota; and SEATTLE, Washington

Canadian Cataloguing in Publication Data

Douthitt, Robin A.
 The Cost of Raising Children in Canada

Includes bibliographical references.
ISBN 0-409-88957-1

1. Child rearing – Economic aspects – Canada.
2. Children – Economic aspects – Canada.
I. Fedyk, Joanne,   II. Title.

HQ769.D68 1990   338.4'76491   C89-095318-X

Sponsoring Editor – Janet Ames
Editor/Cover Design – Bruce Mackenzie
Production – Nancy Harding

PREFACE

In 1983 Professor Robin Douthitt prepared a fact sheet for the Extension Division at the University of Saskatchewan on the cost of raising children in the Prairie region. The response to that publication by families as well as educators and barristers was tremendous. However, those cost estimates had limited applicability as they were derived from a needs based assessment of what low income families *should* spend, rather than actual expenditure data on what middle income families actually *do* spend on their children. By 1985 Professor Joanne Fedyk, then a graduate student, and Professor Douthitt embarked on a pilot study examining the influence of children on Prairie family expenditures that culminated in a proposal to the Social Science and Humanities Research Council of Canada (SSHRCC) to do a similar national study. Research proposal ideas shared with colleagues and family law practitioners met with not only support for the need to do the research but also many requests for copies of findings that were nigh two years from completion. After receiving official word from SSHRCC that they sufficiently shared enthusiasm for this project to fund its execution, the ultimate goal of writing a book on the costs of raising children in Canada was set. This book marks the fulfillment of that objective.

Many professionals have the need to estimate child rearing costs for their clients. With the increased public policy focus on absent parents' obligation to provide adequate economic support for their children, demand for child rearing cost information by family law practitioners has burgeoned. Although parents, mediators, and barristers are most directly involved in establishing child support levels, this area is not their exclusive domain. Increasingly, public policy makers are concerned with such issues, as provincial governments struggle to establish uniformity among themselves for child support awards and as the federal government assesses the adequacy of family allowance payments to defray child rearing costs at all income levels. Family financial planners and home economists have also had a long standing interest in child rearing cost estimates as they assist clients in planning today to meet tomorrow's resource requirements. Our goal was to organize this book in a manner that would be as useful as possible to as many of the helping professions as possible.

Chapter 1 provides an overview for using the book to its best advantage. Part I of the text contains narrative describing our results and walking through some case studies. Rather than organize the book by spending categories such as food, clothing and shelter, each chapter focuses on regional expenditures for all categories of spending. Although this approach does result in some duplication of descriptive narratives, we have found that the increased ease with which most users can access the regional data most salient to their needs outweighs such concerns. However, Chapter 8 does provide a regional overview for the user interested in how expenditures vary across Canada. Tables containing actual child cost information by level of living have been compiled into Part II of the text.

As other authors before us have attested, most books are only made possible with the help and support of many people. First, we would like to thank the Graduate School and the College of Home Economics at the University of Saskatchewan for financial support of our pilot project. The Social Science and Humanities Research Council of Canada also deserves a special thanks not only for funding this important project [#498-85-0005], but also for helping us work out all the usual and not so usual administrative obstacles we faced over the last three years. Finally, we owe thanks to the only people who are probably happier about this project coming to a close than we are, our colleagues and families. All have listened to our endless excuses about how work on this book had to take priority over a meeting, project, or family vacation. Certainly some people are happier than others, since the sweat of their brow went directly into this effort. They include but are not limited to Bonnie, Ellen, Susan, Rachel, and Lenore and to them we dedicate this work.

The authors share responsibility for the accuracy of the results presented and any errors therein. These results and the opinions expressed do not necessarily reflect those of the funding agencies.

Robin A. Douthitt
Joanne M. Fedyk

September 3, 1989

TABLE OF CONTENTS

PART II

CHILD COSTS BY FAMILY INCOME LEVEL BY REGION

CHAPTER 1

INTRODUCTION

The amount of human and monetary resources devoted to raising Canadian children is a matter of great public concern. Individuals sharing in this interest include not only parents, but those who are part of societal infrastructures concerned with providing family support and assistance. Those persons are members of what have become known as the helping professions — financial planning, home economics, family law, public representation, and social work.

Financial planners are interested in knowing how much families spend on children in order to better assist their clients in planning for future financial expenses. Home economists have a broader interest in helping families better manage not only their monetary resources, but also their time and energy, to meet both the direct and opportunity costs of raising children. Members of the legal community primarily apply child cost information to assist clients in child maintenance negotiations. Public representatives, such as government policy makers, are especially concerned with assisting low- to middle-income families meet child rearing costs. They do this in a variety of ways, ranging from enacting programs and policies, to regulating for-profit family service industries such as private day care providers.

Child rearing cost estimates are used by social agencies charged with the responsibility of establishing social assistance payments adequate to meeting children's basic needs. In fact, such agencies have established the family budget guidelines most widely used by all of the helping professions to establish the minimum amount families *should* spend on their children.

Family budget guidelines developed by social service agencies, such as the Social Planning Council of Metropolitan Toronto and the Manitoba Department of Agriculture, are based on a specific "market basket" designed by a panel of experts who identify minimum family needs. Once the market basket is defined, budgets are periodically updated by repricing items in the marketplace. It is this normative methodology that differentiates our study from theirs.

In this book, we provide parents and members of the helping professions with information regarding what lower-middle, middle, and upper-middle income families actually spend on their children. The need for such information is particularly acute in instances where the courts wish to establish a child support award sufficient to ensure that children's standard of living does not suffer as a result of marital dissolution. To date, the primary evidence available to the courts has been the family budget guidelines on what minimum amount families should spend. This book provides information taken from Statistics Canada's Family Expenditure Survey on regional average estimates of what families of different size and income actually spend on their children.

The text is divided into two parts. Part I includes Chapters 2 to 10. Chapter 2 presents an overview of the data used and methods by which we derived our estimates. Chapters 3 through 7 present specific information about child rearing costs of middle-income families by expenditure category for each of five regions: British Columbia; the Prairie provinces (Alberta, Saskatchewan, and Manitoba); Ontario; Quebec; and the Atlantic provinces (New Brunswick, Newfoundland, Nova Scotia, and Prince Edward Island). Chapter 8 summarizes the regional data. Chapters 9 and 10 present case studies with work sheets and specific examples of how to use information presented in the previous chapters. Chapter 9 presents examples of calculating child rearing costs, while Chapter 10 provides examples of applying a discounting factor to calculate present values of child rearing costs. Tables of child rearing cost estimates for families with different income levels are included in Part II.

Readers interested in calculating child rearing costs for either themselves or a specific client should read Chapter 2 and the relevant regional chapter before proceeding to Chapter 9. Detailed information about our methodology and expenditure category definitions are presented in Appendices A and B, respectively.

Part I

CHAPTER 2

DESCRIPTION OF DATA AND METHODS USED

The data used to calculate child rearing cost estimates are from Statistics Canada's 1982 Family Expenditure Survey. Over 10,000 randomly selected families from all over the country were chosen for survey participation. Each family completed a detailed questionnaire regarding its sources of income, family characteristics, and specific expenditures for goods and services purchased in the marketplace. We divided that data by region of the country and selected samples of male-female adult couples under the age of 65 both with and without children. Families were eliminated from the sample if more than one third of their income was from income tested sources,[1] if one or more children were employed full time in the labour force for the entire year, or if a family member were present for only part of the year.

We further divided child rearing cost estimates by level of family income. Income categories were established by ordering our entire sample of family budget data from highest to lowest level of income. Next we divided the sample of families into three equal parts; the third with the lowest incomes, the middle income third, and the third with the highest incomes. In 1988 dollars, the lowest third corresponds to families with gross annual incomes of $15,000 to $30,000 (lower-middle incomes), the middle third to families with gross annual incomes of $30,000 to $45,000 (middle incomes), and the highest third to families with gross annual incomes of $45,000 or more (upper-middle incomes).[2] In Chapters 3 through 7 we report expenditures by middle income families. Comparable data for upper-middle and lower-middle income families are reported in Part II.

The econometric method used to derive cost estimates is one previously reported in Douthitt and Fedyk (1988) and is explained more fully in Appendix A. Rather than estimating the dollar-specific effects of children on family spending, we estimate the share or percentage of income that families allocate towards goods and services due to the presence of children.

Expressing child rearing costs as a percentage of income is advantageous in a number of respects. First, since family expenditures as a percentage of income is fairly constant within income groups,

5

expressing child rearing costs in the same manner provides relatively "timeless" estimates. Family budget guidelines, for example, must be updated annually. Such updating is required not only because they are expressed in nominal dollar amounts, but also because, as relative prices change, the market basket itself must change in order that it reflects the least expensive means by which families can meet their minimum needs. Expressing child rearing costs as a percentage of income automatically abstracts from both the problems of hedging inflation and changing market baskets. Although prices and tastes change, families generally make substitutions in their budgets such that the expenditure remains a fairly constant proportion of total income.

The use of percentage of gross income as a standard for child support awards is also very attractive, in that awards so determined result in support payments that stay current with inflation, thus avoiding the need for litigation by custodial parents in order to receive cost-of-living adjustments. Further, to the extent that real wages of the absent parent increase, child support payments will increase, as do child costs themselves, over the life cycle.

Implicit in applying a percentage formula to absent parents' incomes to calculate their financial responsibility to their children, is that the resulting figure represents only that portion of their income that would have been allocated to child rearing costs had the couple remained together and had the absent parent been the sole economic provider. That is, if *custodial* parents also had an independent source of income while the family was together, the total amount spent on children in the absence of a separation would have exceeded the amount the *absent* parents would be ordered to pay under a child support award based on a percentage of their gross income. Thus, such a formula presumes that custodial parents will similarly share their income in order to meet child rearing costs. If absent parents are to be made responsible for contributing the entire amount that would have otherwise been spent on their children, then their child support obligation would be based on total *family* income prior to their separation. In our examples and case studies, we adhere to the former approach where absent parents only contribute to child support based on their own income.

The econometric model used in this work provides parameters from which child rearing costs for families of various sizes and compositions can be calculated. In order to give concrete examples, we must identify specific family types for analysis. In this work, we provide estimates of child rearing costs for one-, two-, and three- child families.[3] Our prototypical families are assumed to experience a rate of income growth over the life cycle consistent with national trends,[4] to have their first child when the father is 28 and the mother 26, and to have subsequent children at two-year intervals. Although there are virtually an infinite number of other possible family types, these estimates provide a bench mark of what average Canadian families actually spend.

Before proceeding to the regional cost analysis, at least one caveat should be stated. In none of our estimates have we included an allowance for the fact that families may purchase more durable goods, such as automobiles, furniture and major appliances due to a child's presence. Previous authors have included some of these, and thus our estimates will be low *vis-à-vis* those results. More detail on the specific implication of this omission is presented in the regional analyses.

END NOTES

1. Income tested programs include social assistance, unemployment insurance, and other government transfer payments.
2. The highest gross annual family income reported in our Family Expenditures Survey sample was just over $160,000. However, the high income estimates can only be applied with confidence to individuals or families with annual incomes of $100,000 or less.
3. Due to space considerations, we did not include child cost estimates for four-child families. A fourth child's effects are similar to that of the third child and thus third child data may be used to estimate a fourth child's cost. Because regionally, there were so few families in the FES with more than four children, these results cannot be applied with confidence to estimate their child rearing costs.
4. Income streams used in the model simulations were derived using parameter estimates from regressing family income on age of adult male and male's age squared using the entire national sample of FES families.

CHAPTER 3

CHILD REARING COSTS: BRITISH COLUMBIA

This chapter presents information on child rearing costs and how British Columbia middle-income families manage their resources to meet those costs. On average, over the life cycle, two-child families spend about 17% of gross income to meet child rearing costs. This does not include additional spending for child care, housing, or durable goods, such as vehicles, household furniture, appliances, and recreational equipment necessitated by the addition of children to the family. The addition of a child to a British Columbia family causes increases in expenditures for food at home, clothing, utilities, transportation, education, household operation and health care.

Families meet the cost of raising children in many ways, including increasing their incomes, increasing the amount of time spent in household work, reallocating income from other expenditures to child goods, or decreasing their savings. We examine the latter two strategies in this study. First, we find that British Columbia families spend less for food away from home, recreation, adult goods such as tobacco and alcohol, parental clothing, and gifts in order to meet child rearing costs. Second, British Columbia families with children also save less than their childless counterparts. Families with two children save about 22% of gross income during the child rearing years compared to an average savings rate of 26% by childless couples over the same period.

The remainder of the chapter presents more detailed information and examples regarding British Columbia child cost estimates. Immediately following are summary and itemized cost estimates by expenditure category over the life cycle. Housing and child care estimates are considered apart from other expenditures as they are often given special treatment in financial planning and court-awarded child support orders. We conclude with a discussion of how British Columbia families reduce their savings in order to meet child rearing costs. The data tables described in the following sections are found in Part II. Similar data for upper-middle income British Columbia families is found in Tables 1-6 in Part II, while data for lower-middle income families is given in Tables 13-18 also in Part II.

9

EXPENDITURE ESTIMATES

Table 7 reports percentages of gross annual income allocated to meeting child costs, *excluding* housing, durable goods, and child care. On average, the marginal cost of the first, second and third child for middle-income families is about 9, 11, and 9% of gross income. Over the life cycle, this amounts to an average of about 9, 17, and 23% of gross income[1] for one-, two- and three- child families respectively. By excluding major durable items like housing and appliances from the cost estimates, we find no overall economies of scale present. Costs as a percentage of gross income steadily increase as a child ages, reflecting the fact that, during the later stages of the life cycle, meeting children's physical requirements demands less household work time and more material goods. Not only do total outlays on behalf of children increase, but the allocation of child rearing costs among specific spending categories also varies over the life cycle.[2] The next sections summarize these trends.

Food at Home

Table 8 presents information on the percentages of annual child rearing costs allocated by middle-income families to specific spending categories for each child. Food at home comprises the largest portion of child rearing costs in every year of the life cycle. It consists of food purchased from stores, and does *not* include food purchased in restaurants and fast food outlets. (See Appendix B for detailed expenditure accounts.) Expenditures for food at home for an only child average 55% of total child rearing costs over the life cycle (Table 8). Although expenditures for food at home first increase and then decrease as a percentage of total annual child costs over time, the absolute dollar outlays increase steadily. This trend simply reflects the fact that child costs increase at an annual rate greater than spending for food at home during the teen years. For example, when the first child is five years of age, 62% of her total cost that year is composed of food costs. If family income equals $20,000 in that year, total child costs would amount to about $1,400 (7% annual cost (from Table 7) times $20,000); and food costs would equal $868. By the child's sixteenth year, food costs constitute only 51% of her annual cost; however, total costs since the fifth year have increased by 3%, and income will have increased by approximately 24% (assuming 2%/year real income growth rate), such that annual food at home costs would be about $1,265 (10% annual cost (from Table 7) times a gross annual income of $24,800).

Food at home expenditures average 57 and 51% (Table 8) of the total costs for second and third children, respectively, over the life cycle. As a percentage of annual costs, food at home increases, then decreases over time, a trend similar to that of the one-child family.

Clothing

Clothing composes the second largest portion of child rearing costs. It includes outlays for both children's clothing and adult clothing purchased for children age 13 and older. Expenditures for outerwear, accessories and footwear are also included in this category. Expenditures for clothing for an only child average 14% of total child rearing costs over the life cycle (Table 8). Both the percentage of annual child costs and the dollar outlay for clothing steadily increase over time. If, as in our previous example, annual child costs for one five-year-old child amount to 7% of gross income or $1,400, then clothing costs in that year amount to 13% (Table 8) of those costs, about $182.

Clothing expenditures for each of the second and third children average 18 and 30% respectively of their total child rearing costs over the life cycle. Although a larger portion of their costs are attributable to clothing expenditures, the percentage of second and third children's annual costs attributable to clothing, unlike the first child, both increase and decrease over the life cycle.

Education and Related Expenditures

Education-related expenses include spending on tuition, lessons, school supplies, and reading materials such as books and magazine subscriptions. (See Appendix B for detailed expenditure accounts.)

Spending on education for a one-child family averages 5% of total child rearing costs (Table 8). Education as a percentage of total costs steadily increases as the child ages. No significant additional education expenditures are made for the second child until after the oldest child leaves home. Because during the early years the two-child family allocates no additional funds to educational expenses (over what they would have spent had they only one child), the average expenditure as a percentage of the total cost over the life cycle is lower than that of the first child, at 1%.

No significant additional allocations to educational goods and services are made until the third child reaches age 14. Over the life cycle, approximately 1% of the third child's total cost is attributable to educational expenses.

Transportation

This category consists of spending for the operation of automobiles and trucks for personal use including fuel, maintenance and repairs, insurance and licence fees. Additional expenditures include outlays for bus, cab, trains, and plane fares. (See Appendix B for detailed expenditure accounts.) Expenditures on the purchase of vehicles are *not* included in transportation. Vehicle purchase is considered to be an investment and is included in savings (see discussion of Table 12).

Spending on transportation composes about 7% of the total cost of raising the first child (Table 8). Transportation expenditures, as a proportion of annual costs, are highest in the early and latter years of the life cycle. Initially, the proportion of annual costs allocated to transportation declines until the first child reaches school age, and thereafter increases.

Transportation expenditures compose only a small part of the total costs of second and third children (Table 8). Spending on transportation as a percentage of the second and third child's costs are significant when children are young, significantly emerge again as each nears driving age and increase steadily thereafter. However, over the 18-year period, transportation expenditures compose only 5 and 2% of total child rearing costs for the second and third child, respectively.

Utilities

Utility-related expenses compose the third largest portion of the first, second, and third child's rearing costs. This category includes expenditures for water, heating fuel, electricity, and telephone. (See Appendix B for detailed expenditure accounts.) Expenditures for utilities attributable to the presence of an only child average 7% of total child rearing costs over the life cycle (Table 8). Although the annual dollar outlay remains fairly constant, utilities as a percentage of annual child costs decline over the life cycle.

Utility spending trends attributable to the presence of the second and third child average 8 and 7% respectively. A decreasing percentage of both the second and third child's annual costs are spent on utilities.

Health Care

This category includes money spent for eye glasses or eye care, pharmaceutical products, dental care (orthodontics, etc.), and health insurance premiums. (See Appendix B for detailed expenditure accounts.) In 1982, for a $32 monthly fee, the British Columbia government provided routine dental care for children under the age of 14. The cost of routine eye care, including contact lens fittings, was also part of this coverage.

Expenditures for the first, second, and third child's health care average each about 4% of their total child rearing costs over the life cycle (Table 8). As a percentage of annual costs, health care expenditures peak when children are around 13 years of age, and decline thereafter.

Household Operations

Household operation makes up 4% of the child rearing costs for one child. For each of the second and third child, household operation composes the smallest portion of child rearing costs. It includes outlays for household cleaning supplies, pet supplies, household and clothing textiles, services related to furnishings and clothing, plus personal care supplies and services. (See Appendix B for detailed expenditure accounts.)

Expenditures for household operations average 1% of the second and third child's total cost over the life cycle (Table 8).

HOUSING

As mentioned in the introduction, none of the previously discussed child cost estimates include an allowance for housing. It is being treated as a separate budget item, similar to court cases where child support and matrimonial property awards are concurrently determined. Of particular interest are those instances where a matrimonial home is included in jointly held matrimonial property. Although in most situations the custodial parent is allowed to remain in the home, final ownership of the property may be retained by either or both parents, depending on the outcome of mediation. In cases where the custodial parent is also the owner of the property, side deals for fair compensation of housing costs attributable to the child may be necessary.

For these reasons, we examine housing costs apart from other child rearing costs. Further, because court child support awards differentially compensate custodial parents who rent their residence from those who share in ownership of a matrimonial home, and because analysis has revealed that renters incur different costs than owners, we will discuss each separately.

Owned Housing

Our measure of owned housing costs represents a departure from its traditional treatment in the literature. Most researchers who have used consumer expenditure data to examine family budgeting adopt the definition of owned housing expenditures used by the data collection agency. For example, Statistics Canada includes outlays for maintenance and repairs, property tax, insurance and mortgage interest in its housing definition. Most notably excluded from this definition are mortgage principal payments. While, in a strict accounting sense, these payments actually represent a net change in assets, for purposes of planning for meeting child rearing costs, most families require access to annual estimates of how much money they need to set aside to meet the increased demand for housing necessitated by the child's presence, regardless of whether that allocation goes to mortgage interest or principal. Thus, the academic distinction between mortgage interest and principal is less important than providing families in varying circumstances with some idea of what they might actually spend for total housing.

Our definition of owned housing expenditures includes all of the traditionally defined components as well as payments to mortgage principal. This approach is not intended to diminish the important role of owned housing equity accrual as a financial planning tool, but rather emphasizes the need to develop alternative accounting measures appropriate to the purpose of the planning exercise, e.g., financial planning to meet child rearing costs versus retirement consumption needs.

Although we discuss the independent influence of children on housing expenditures of home owners and renters, in fact, the presence of children in British Columbia households significantly influences the probability of home ownership. For example, the addition of a child (the first) to the family increases the probability of home ownership by about 28%. [3]

Table 9 presents information about the percentage of gross income that middle income British Columbia home owners spend for housing. Overall, the percentage of income allocated to housing declines with family size. This does not necessarily imply that families with more children have homes of lesser value than their counterparts with fewer children, but that they reallocate their resources, perhaps by financing their mortgage over a longer period, such that their monthly housing outlay is reduced.

It is reasonable to assume that families move into larger and more expensive living accommodations as the result of the presence of children. To estimate the amount of money families can plan on paying for this additional space, we examined the average cost per room paid by British Columbia home owners. On average, the addition of a room necessitates an increase in housing expenditures by about 8%, or about 1% of gross income. For simplicity, we will assume that each child will require additional space the equivalent of one room. *Thus, for home owners, 1% per child should be added to annual child rearing costs to cover increased housing requirements necessitated by the child's presence.*

Rental Housing

Table 9 also presents data regarding the percentages of income that British Columbia renters of different family types allocate to housing.

Like home owners, the percentage of income allocated to housing declines slightly with family size. This seemingly anomalous result has been found in previous studies and explained by the fact that large rental housing is not readily available. Thus as family size increases, families who continue to rent are less able to move to a larger, and thus more costly, unit.

An important distinction between expenditures by renters versus owners, is not only that over time owners are accumulating assets, but also that owners pay a smaller and smaller share of gross income to meet housing costs as their fixed mortgage payment composes a smaller and smaller share of annual income. Renters, on the other hand, face allocating a relatively constant share of income to housing over the life cycle, as rental payments increase, keeping pace with increases in the overall cost-of-living index.

Our data reveals that British Columbia renters spend about 5% more on housing (or 1% of annual gross income) by increasing their house or apartment size by one room. *Thus, for renters, 1% per child should be added to annual child rearing costs to cover increased housing requirements necessitated by the child's presence.*

CHILD CARE

Child care expenses are a second category of expenditures that we have identified to study apart from other child rearing costs. There are differences in expenditures across family types depending on whether one or both parents are employed in the labour force. Our definition of child care expenditures include outlays for babysitting and child care, both in and outside the home, as long as money was not paid to an immediate household member.

Table 10 presents information on the percentage of gross income that various sizes of families spend on child care according to whether one or both parents are employed outside the home. Over an 11-year period, families with two children where both parents are employed spend about 2% of gross income for day care. One-, two-, and three-child families, where only one parent is employed, spend less than 1% for child care.

TOTAL CHILD REARING COSTS

Table 11 presents a summary of total child rearing costs as a percentage of gross income for families who own their own home and where both parents are employed in the labour force. On average, families with one child spend about 12% of their gross income to meet child rearing costs, two-child families about 20%, and three-child families about 27%. Small economies to scale are noted for the second child, and for the third child. Since renters pay about the same for housing on a per room basis, their average costs, including day care if both parents are employed, would be similar to that of home owners.

OTHER DURABLE GOODS

Our analysis has excluded outlays for durable goods that may be attributable to the presence of children. Omitted are expenditures for recreational vehicles, boats, new and used automobiles, household furnishings and appliances. This is a departure from previous studies that included all the above in various expenditure categories. In a previous study, the authors found that about 9% of an average Canadian family's expenditures could be classified as going toward the purchase of durable goods, 5% of which is attributable to vehicle purchase. While childless couples appeared to allocate a fairly constant share of total expenditures for durable goods over the life cycle, peaks in the budget shares two-child families allocated to durable goods occurred in each year that a child was born, and at the stage in the life cycle where children reached driving age. One can easily speculate on the nature of spending behaviour that would cause these differences.

Again, since previous studies of child rearing costs included durable outlays in their expenditure definitions, our child rearing costs will be less than theirs. To the extent durable purchases are made for the benefit of children, and that these assets are depreciated by the child's use, our estimates will underestimate the costs of children. More technically stated, if due to depreciation attributable to the child's use, net asset accrual is less than what it would have been had the child not benefitted from or used the durable goods, our estimates will understate the cost of raising children.

MEETING CHILD REARING COSTS

Seldom is the arrival of a child accompanied by an increase in income sufficient to meet the additional demands placed on family resources. Families meet these demands in several ways. First, they may increase the amount of time spent in the labour force. This strategy is more common during the later stages of the life cycle when the child's needs are less time and more goods intensive. During the early stages of the life cycle, however, it is more common that family income decreases as parents choose to meet the demands of child rearing by increasing the amount of time spent working in the home.

Another strategy used by parents to meet child rearing costs is to reduce certain expenditures as compared to what they would have spent had a child not been present in the household. British Columbian families tend to spend less for food eaten away from home, recreation, adult goods such as tobacco and alcohol, parental clothing, and gifts in order to meet child rearing costs.

Finally, families may choose to meet the costs of child rearing by saving less; that is, foregoing future consumption. Table 12 presents information regarding the savings patterns of various families. Change in savings includes not only contributions to conventional measures such as cash held in banks, contributions to Registered Retirement Savings Plans (RRSPs) and other financial assets, but also allocations towards the purchase of durable goods such as vehicles, recreational equipment, furniture, and appliances.

On average, families with children save less than their childless counterparts. Childless couples on average save 26% of gross income and tend to steadily increase their savings rates over the life cycle, while couples with one, two and three children save an average of 23, 22, and 21% respectively and experience both upward and downward savings trends over similar stages of the life cycle.

END NOTES

1. Over an 18-, 20-, and 22- year life cycle, respectively.
2. Throughout the text, when reference is made to families with more than one child, the implicit assumption is that children are spaced two years apart.
3. These estimates were derived by calculating marginal effects from probit regressions on a dichotomous dependent variable indicating whether or not the family owned their own home.

CHAPTER 4

CHILD REARING COSTS: PRAIRIE REGION

This chapter presents information on child rearing costs and how Prairie (provinces of Alberta, Saskatchewan, and Manitoba), middle-income families manage their resources to meet those costs. On average, over the life cycle, two-child families spend about 17% of gross income to meet child rearing costs. This does not include additional spending for child care, housing, or durable goods, such as vehicles, household furniture, appliances, and recreational equipment necessitated by the addition of children to the family. The addition of a child to Prairie families causes increases in expenditures for food at home, clothing, utilities, transportation, education, household operation and health care.

Families meet the cost of raising children in many ways, including increasing their incomes, increasing the amount of time spent in household work, reallocating income from other expenditures to child goods, or decreasing their savings. We examine the latter two strategies in this study. First, we find that Prairie families spend less for food away from home, recreation, adult goods such as tobacco and alcohol, parental clothing, and gifts in order to meet child rearing costs. Second, Prairie families with children also save less than their childless counterparts. Families with two children save about 10% of gross income during the child rearing years, compared to an average savings rate of 12% by childless couples over the same period.

The remainder of the chapter presents more detailed information about expenditures made by Prairie families on behalf of their children. Immediately following are summary and itemized cost estimates by expenditure category over the life cycle. Housing and child care estimates are considered apart from other expenditures as they are often given special treatment in financial planning and court-awarded child support orders. We conclude with a discussion of how Prairie families reduce their savings in order to meet child rearing costs. The data tables described in the following sections are found in Part II. Similar data for upper-middle income Prairie families is found in Tables 19-24 in Part II, while data for lower-middle income Prairies families is given in Tables 31-36 in Part II.

EXPENDITURE ESTIMATES

Table 25 reports percentages of gross annual income allocated to meet each child's cost, *excluding* housing, durable goods, and child care expenditures. Assuming that children are spaced two years apart, we find that the marginal cost of first, second and third children for middle-income families is about 9, 9, and 10% of gross income. Over the life cycle, this amounts to an average of about 9, 17, and 23% of gross income[1] for one-, two-, and three-child families respectively. By excluding major durable items like housing and appliances from the cost estimates, we find no overall economies of scale present. Costs as a percentage of gross income increase as children age, reflecting the fact that, during the later stages of the life cycle, meeting children's physical requirements demands less household work time and more material goods. Not only do total outlays on behalf of children increase, but the allocation of child rearing costs among specific spending categories also varies over the life cycle.[2] The next sections summarize these trends.

Food at Home

Table 26 presents information on the percentages of annual child rearing costs allocated to specific spending categories for each child. Food at home comprises the largest portion of child rearing costs in every year of the life cycle. It consists of food purchased from stores, and does *not* include food purchased in restaurants and fast food outlets. (See Appendix B for detailed expenditure accounts.)

Expenditures for food at home for an only child average 54% of total child rearing costs over the life cycle (Table 26). Although expenditures for food at home first increase and then decrease as a percentage of total annual child costs over time, the absolute dollar outlays increase steadily. This trend simply reflects the fact that child costs increase at an annual rate greater than spending for food at home during the teen years.

For example, when the first child is five years of age, 60% of her total cost that year is composed of food costs. If family income equals $20,000 in that year, total child costs would amount to about $1,600 (8% annual cost (from Table 25) times $20,000), and food costs would equal $960. By the child's sixteenth year, food costs constitute only 43% of her annual cost; however, total costs since the fifth year have increased by 4% and income will have increased by approximately 24% (assuming 2%/year real income growth rate), such that annual food at home costs would be about $1,280 (12% annual cost (from Table 25) times a gross annual income of $24,800).

Food at home expenditures average 59 and 53% (Table 26) of the total costs for the second and third child, respectively, over the life cycle. As a percentage of annual costs, food at home increases then decreases over time, a trend similar to that of the one-child family.

Clothing

Clothing expenditures make up the second largest portion of child rearing costs. It includes outlays for both children's clothing and adult clothing purchased for children age 13 and older. Expenditures for outerwear, accessories and footwear are also included in this category.

Expenditures for clothing for an only child average 13% of total child rearing costs over the life cycle (Table 26). Both the percentage of annual child costs and the absolute dollar outlay for clothing steadily increase over time. If, as in our previous example, annual child costs for one five-year-old child amount to 8% of gross income, or $2,600, then clothing costs in that year amount to 12% (Table 26) of those costs, about $312.

Clothing expenditures for each of the second and third children average 19 and 29% respectively of their total child rearing costs over the life cycle. Although a larger portion of their costs are attributable to clothing expenditures, the percentage of second and third children's annual costs attributable to clothing, unlike the first child, declines over the life cycle while other siblings remain in the household.

Education and Related Expenditures

This category includes spending on tuition, lessons, school supplies, and reading materials such as books and magazine subscriptions. (See Appendix B for detailed expenditure accounts.)

Spending on education for a one-child family averages 8% of total child rearing costs (Table 26). Education as a percentage of total costs steadily increases as the child ages. No significant additional education expenditures are made for the second child until she is eight years of age. Thereafter, educational spending for the second child follows an increasing trend, increasing at a faster rate than that observed for the first child. Because during the early years the two-child family allocates no additional funds to educational expenses (over what they would have spent had they only one child), the average expenditure as a percentage of the total cost over the life cycle is lower than that of the first child, at 6%.

Spending for the third child follows a pattern similar to that of the second child. No significant additional allocations to educational goods and services are made until the third child reaches age 11. Like the second child, educational expenditures as a percentage of total annual costs increase while other siblings are present in the household. Over the life cycle, approximately 4% of the third child's total cost is attributable to educational expenses.

Transportation

Transportation expenditures are comprised of spending for the operation of automobiles and trucks for personal use including fuel, maintenance and repairs, insurance and licence fees. Additional expenditures include outlays for bus, cab, trains, and plane fares. (See Appendix B for detailed expenditure accounts.) Expenditures on the purchase of vehicles are *not* included in transportation. Vehicle purchase is considered to be an investment and is included in savings. (See discussion of Table 30).

Spending on transportation constitutes 8% of the total cost of raising the first child (Table 26). Transportation expenditures, as a proportion of annual costs, are highest in the early and latter years of the life cycle. Initially, the proportion of annual costs allocated to transportation declines until the first child reaches school age, and thereafter increases.

Transportation expenditures compose only a small part of the total costs of second and third children (Table 26). Spending on transportation as a percentage of the second and third children costs occurs as each nears driving age, and increases steadily. However, over the 18-year period, transportation expenditures compose only 2% of total child rearing costs for the second and third child.

Utilities

This category includes expenditures for water, heating fuel, electricity, and telephone. (See Appendix B for detailed expenditure accounts.)

Expenditures for utilities attributable to the presence of an only child average 10% of total child rearing costs over the life cycle (Table 26). Although the annual dollar outlay remains fairly constant, utilities as a percentage of annual child costs declines over the life cycle.

Utility spending trends attributable to the presence of the second and third child average 8 and 4% respectively. Although a decreasing percentage of the second child's annual costs are spent on utilities, an increasing percentage of the third child's annual costs are allocated to utilities, mostly during the teen years.

Health Care

Outlays for health care include money spent for eye glasses or eye care, pharmaceutical products, dental care (orthodontics, etc.), and health insurance premiums. (See Appendix B for detailed expenditure accounts.)

In 1982, for a monthly premium of $19, the province of Alberta provided family health care that included coverage for routine dental care and one eye examination per year. Neither orthodontic treatments, eye glass frames, nor lens costs were included under this coverage. Similar benefits were provided by both the Saskatchewan and Manitoba governments at no charge to families. However, in Manitoba, dental coverage was only provided for children 15 years of age and under; and since 1982 Saskatchewan has further restricted its child health care coverage. Thus, our calculations likely underestimate average current health care outlays by Prairie parents on behalf of their children.

Expenditures for a first and third child's health care average for each about 2% of their total child rearing costs over the life cycle (Table 26). As a percentage of annual costs, health care expenditures peak when children are 9 to 13 years of age and decline thereafter.

Health care expenditures for a second child average 1% of their total child rearing costs over the life cycle. Like the first and third child, the second child's health care expenses, as a proportion of annual costs, are minimal during the pre-school stage of the life cycle, and emerge as significant only during the teen years.

Household Operations

Household operation makes up a very small portion of the costs for each child. It includes outlays for household cleaning supplies, pet supplies, household and clothing textiles, services related to furnishings and clothing plus personal care supplies and services. (See Appendix B for detailed expenditure accounts.) Expenditures for household operations average 2, 1 and 1% of the first, second, and third child's total cost over the life cycle (Table 26). Household operations do not emerge as a significant expenditure item until children reach 9 to 13 years of age. Once children reach their teens, household operations remain steady at around 4 to 5% of annual costs.

HOUSING

As mentioned in the introduction, none of the previously discussed child cost estimates include an allowance for housing costs. It is being treated as a separate budget item similar to court cases where child support and matrimonial property awards are concurrently determined. Of particular interest are those instances where a matrimonial home is included in jointly held matrimonial property.

Although in most situations the custodial parent is allowed to remain in the home, final ownership of the property may be retained by either or both parents, depending on the outcome of mediation. In circumstances where the custodial parent is also the owner of the property, side deals for fair compensation of housing costs attributable to the child may be needed.

For these reasons, we examine housing costs apart from other child rearing costs. Further, because court child support awards differentially compensate custodial parents who rent their residence from those who share in ownership of a matrimonial home, and because analysis has revealed that renters incur different costs than owners, we will discuss each separately.

Owned Housing

Our measure of owned housing costs represents a departure from its traditional treatment in the literature. Most researchers who have used consumer expenditure data to examine family budgeting adopt the definition of owned housing expenditures used by the data collection agency. For example, Statistics Canada includes outlays for maintenance and repairs, property tax, insurance and mortgage interest in its housing definition. Most notably excluded from this definition are mortgage principal payments. While in a strict accounting sense these payments actually represent a net change in assets, for purposes of planning for meeting child rearing costs, most families require access to annual estimates of how much money they need to set aside to meet the increased demand for housing necessitated by the child's presence, regardless of whether that allocation goes to mortgage interest or principal. Thus, the academic distinction between mortgage interest and principal is less important than providing families in varying circumstances with some idea of what they might actually spend for total housing.

Our definition of owned housing expenditures includes all of the traditionally defined components as well as payments to mortgage principal. This approach is not intended to diminish the important role of owned housing equity accrual as a financial planning tool, but rather emphasizes the need to develop alternative accounting measures appropriate to the purpose of the planning exercise, e.g., financial planning to meet child rearing costs versus retirement consumption needs.

Although we discuss the independent influence of children on both home owners' and renters' housing expenditures, in fact, the presence of children in Prairie households significantly influences the probability of home ownership. For example, the addition of a child (the first) to the family increases the probability of home ownership by about 32%.[3]

Table 27 presents information about the percentage of gross income that Prairie home owners spend for housing. Overall, the percentage of income allocated to housing declines slightly with family size. This does not necessarily imply that families with more children have homes of the same or lesser value as their counterparts with fewer children, but that they reallocate their resources, perhaps by financing their mortgage over a longer period, such that their monthly housing outlay is equivalent.

It is reasonable to assume that families move into larger and more expensive living accommodations as the result of the presence of children. To estimate the amount of money families can plan on paying for this additional space, we examined the average cost per room paid by Prairie home owners. On average, the addition of a room necessitates an increase in housing expenditures of about 9% or about 1% of gross income. For simplicity, we will assume that each child will require additional space the equivalent of one room. *Thus, for home owners, 1% per child should be added to annual child rearing costs to cover increased housing requirements necessitated by the child's presence.*

Rental Housing

Table 27 also presents data on the percentages of income that Prairie renters of different family types allocate to housing. The percentage of income allocated to rental housing is negatively related to family size. This seemingly anomalous result has been found in previous studies and explained by the fact that large rental housing is not readily available. Thus, as family size increases, families who continue to rent are less able to move to a larger, and thus more costly, unit.

An important distinction between expenditures by renters versus owners is not only that, over time, owners are accumulating assets, but also that owners pay a smaller and smaller share of gross income to meet housing costs as their fixed mortgage payment composes a smaller and smaller share of annual income. Renters, on the other hand, face allocating a relatively constant share of income to housing over the life cycle as rental payments increase, keeping pace with increases in the overall cost of living index.

Our data indicate that Prairie renters spend about 7% more on housing (or 1% of annual gross income) by increasing their house or apartment size by one room. *Thus, for renters, 1% per child should be added to annual child rearing costs to cover increased housing requirements due to child's presence.*

CHILD CARE

Child care expenses are a second category of expenditures that we have identified to study apart from other child rearing costs. There are differences in expenditures across family types depending on whether one or both parents are employed in the labour force. Our definition of child care expenditures includes outlays for babysitting and child care, both in and outside the home, as long as money was not paid to an immediate household member.

Table 28 presents information on the percentage of gross income that various sizes of families spend on child care according to whether one or both parents are employed outside the home. Over an 11-year period, families where both parents are employed spend about 3% of gross income for daycare. One- and two-child families where only one parent is employed spend less than 1% for child care while three-child families spend about 1% of gross income.

TOTAL CHILD REARING COSTS

Table 29 presents a summary of total child rearing costs as a percentage of gross income for families who own their own home and where both parents are employed in the labour force. On average, families with one child spend about 12% of their gross income to meet child rearing costs, two-child families about 20% and three-child families about 28%. Small economies to scale are noted for the second child, but not for the third child. Since renters pay about the same for housing on a per room basis, their average costs, including day care if both parents are employed, would be similar to that of home owners.

OTHER DURABLE GOODS

Nowhere in our analysis have we included outlays for durable goods that may be attributable to the presence of children. Omitted are expenditures for recreational vehicles, boats, new and used automobiles, household furnishings and appliances. This is a departure from previous studies that included all the above in various expenditure categories. In a previous study, the authors found that about 9% of an average Canadian family's expenditures could be classified as going toward the purchase of durable goods, 5% of which is attributable to vehicle purchase. While childless couples appeared to allocate a fairly constant share of total expenditures over the life cycle for durable goods, peaks in the budget shares that two-child families allocated to durable goods occurred in each year where a child was born, and at the stage in the life cycle where children reached driving age. One can easily speculate on the nature of spending behaviour that would cause these differences.

Again, since previous studies of child rearing costs included durable outlays in their expenditure definitions, our child rearing costs will be less than theirs. To the extent durable purchases are made for the benefit of children and that the assets are depreciated by the child's use, our estimates will underestimate the costs of children. More technically stated, if due to depreciation attributable to the child's use, net asset accrual is less than what it would have been had the child not benefitted from or used the durable goods, our estimates will understate the cost of raising children.

MEETING CHILD REARING COSTS

Seldom is the arrival of a child accompanied by an increase in income sufficient to meet the additional demands placed on family resources. Families meet these demands in several ways. First, they may increase the amount of time spent in the labour force. This strategy is more common during the later stages of the life cycle when the child's needs are less time and more goods intensive. During the early stages of the life cycle, however, it is more common that family income decreases as parents choose to meet the demands of child rearing by increasing the amount of time spent working in the home.

Another strategy used by parents to meet child rearing costs is to reduce certain expenditures as compared to what they would have spent had a child not been present in the household. Prairie families tend to spend less for food eaten away from home, recreation, adult goods such as tobacco and alcohol, parental clothing, and gifts in order to meet child rearing costs.

Finally, families may choose to meet the costs of child rearing by saving less; that is, foregoing future consumption. Table 30 presents information regarding the savings patterns of various families. Change in savings includes not only contributions to conventional measures such as cash held in banks, contributions to Registered Retirement Savings Plans (RRSPs) and other financial assets, but also allocations towards the purchase of durable goods such as vehicles, recreational equipment, furniture, and appliances.

On average, families with children save less than their childless counterparts. Childless couples save an average of 12% and tend to steadily increase their savings rates over the life cycle, while couples with one and two children save less and experience both upward and downward savings trends over similar stages of the life cycle. One-and two-child couples save about 10% of gross income. The addition of a third child results in a small increase (1%) in the average savings rate, due in part to increased demand for durable goods.

END NOTES

1. Over an 18-, 20- and 22- year life cycle, respectively.
2. Throughout the text, when reference is made to families with more than one child, the implicit assumption is that children are spaced two years apart.
3. These estimates were derived by calculating marginal effects from probit regressions on a dichotomous dependent variable indicating whether or not the family owned their own home.

CHAPTER 5

CHILD REARING COSTS: ONTARIO

This chapter presents information on child rearing costs and how Ontario middle-income families manage their resources to meet those costs. On average, over the life cycle, two-child families spend about 18% of gross income to meet child rearing costs. This does not include additional spending for child care, housing, or durable goods, such as vehicles, household furniture, appliances, and recreational equipment necessitated by the addition of children to the family. The addition of a child to Ontario families causes increases in expenditures for food at home, clothing, utilities, transportation, education, household operation and health care.

Families meet the cost of raising children in many ways, including increasing their incomes, increasing the amount of time spent in household work, reallocating income from other expenditures to child goods, or decreasing their savings. We examine the latter two strategies in this study. First, we find that Ontario families spend less for food away from home, recreation, adult goods such as tobacco and alcohol, parental clothing, and gifts in order to meet child rearing costs. Second, Ontario families with children also save less than their childless counterparts. Families with two children save about 17% of gross income during the child rearing years, compared to an average savings rate of 29% by childless couples over the same period.

The remainder of the chapter presents more detailed information about expenditures made by Ontario families on behalf of their children. Immediately following are summary and itemized cost estimates by expenditure category over the life cycle. Housing and child care estimates are considered apart from other expenditures as they are often given special treatment in financial planning and court-awarded child support orders. We conclude with a discussion of how Ontario families reduce their savings in order to meet child rearing costs. The data tables described in the following sections are found in Part II. Similar data for upper-middle income Ontario families is found in Tables 37-42 in Part II, while data for lower-middle income families is given in Tables 49-54 also in Part II.

EXPENDITURE ESTIMATES

Table 43 reports percentages of gross annual income allocated to meet each child's cost, *excluding* housing, durable goods, and child care expenditures. Assuming that children are spaced two years apart, we find that over the life cycle, the marginal cost of the first, second, and third child for middle income families is about 10-11% of gross income. Over the life cycle, this amounts to about 11, 18, and 25% of gross income[1] for one-, two-, and three-child families respectively. By excluding major durable items like housing and appliances from the cost estimates, we find only small economies of scale present. Costs as a percentage of gross income steadily increase as children age, reflecting the fact that, during the later stages of the life cycle, meeting children's physical requirements demands less household work time and more material goods. Not only do total outlays on behalf of children increase, but the allocation of child rearing costs among specific spending categories also varies over the life cycle.[2] The next sections summarize these trends.

Food at Home

Table 44 presents information on the percentages of annual child rearing costs allocated to specific spending categories for each child. Food at home comprises the largest portion of child rearing costs in every year of the life cycle. It consists of food purchased from stores, and does *not* include food purchased in restaurants and fast food outlets. (See Appendix B for detailed expenditure accounts.)

Expenditures for food at home for an only child average 45% of total child rearing costs over the life cycle (Table 44). Although expenditures for food at home first increase and then decrease as a percentage of total annual child costs over time, the absolute dollar outlays increase steadily. This trend simply reflects the fact that child costs increase at an annual rate greater than spending for food at home during the teen years.

For example, when the first child is five years of age, 49% of her total cost that year is composed of food costs. If family income equals $20,000 in that year, total child costs would amount to about $1,800 (9% annual cost (from Table 43) times $20,000), and food costs would equal $882. By the child's sixteenth year food costs compose only 37% of her annual cost; however, total costs since the fifth year have increased by 4% and income will have increased by approximately 24% (assuming 2%/year real income growth rate) such that annual food at home costs would be about $1,193 (13% annual cost (from Table 43) times a gross annual income of $24,800).

Food at home expenditures average 52 and 48% (Table 44) of the total costs for second and third children, respectively, over the life cycle. As a percentage of annual costs, food at home increases then decreases over time, a trend similar to that of the one-child family.

Clothing

Clothing expenditures make up the third largest portion of first child, and the second largest portion of second and third child's rearing costs. It includes outlays for both children's clothing and adult clothing purchased for children age 13 and older. Expenditures for outerwear, accessories and footwear are also included in this category.

Expenditures for clothing for an only child average 11% of total child rearing costs over the life cycle (Table 44). The absolute dollar outlay for clothing steadily increases over time. If, as in our previous example, annual child costs for one five-year-old child amount to 9% of gross income or $1,800, then clothing costs in that year amount to 11% (Table 44) of those costs, about $198. Clothing expenditures for each of the second and third children average 18 and 29% respectively of their total child rearing costs over the life cycle.

Education and Related Expenditures

Education-related expenses include spending on tuition, lessons, school supplies, and reading materials such as books and magazine subscriptions. (See Appendix B for detailed expenditure accounts.)

Spending on education for a one-child family averages 10% of total child rearing costs (Table 44). No significant additional education expenditures are made for the second child between ages 5 and 10. Thereafter, educational spending for the second child follows an increasing trend, increasing at a faster rate than that observed for the first child. Because during the middle years the two-child family allocates no additional funds to educational expenses (over what they would have spent had they only one child), the average expenditure as a percentage of the total cost over the life cycle is lower than that of the first child, at 5%.

No significant additional allocations to educational goods and services are made for the third child until she reaches age 15. Over the life cycle, approximately 3% of the third child's total cost is attributable to educational expenses.

Transportation

Transportation expenditures are comprised of spending for the operation of automobiles and trucks for personal use including fuel, maintenance and repairs, insurance and licence fees. Additional expenditures include outlays for bus, cab, trains, and plane fares. (See Appendix B for detailed expenditure accounts.) Expenditures on the purchase of vehicles are *not* included in transportation. Vehicle purchase is considered to be an investment and is included in savings (see discussion of Table 48).

Spending on transportation composes about 11% of the total cost of raising the first child (Table 44). Transportation expenditures, as a proportion of annual costs, are highest in the early and latter years of the life cycle. Initially, the proportion of annual costs allocated to transportation declines until the first child reaches eight years of age, and thereafter increases.

Transportation expenditures compose only a small part of the total costs of second and third children (Table 44). Spending on transportation as a percentage of the second and third child's costs occurs as each nears driving age and increases annually. However, over the 18-year period, transportation expenditures compose only 3% of total child rearing costs for the second and third child.

Utilities

Utility related expenses compose the second largest portion of the first child's cost and the third largest portion of the second and third child's rearing costs. This category includes expenditures for water, heating fuel, electricity, and telephone. (See Appendix B for detailed expenditure accounts.)

Expenditures for utilities attributable to the presence of an only child average 12% of total child rearing costs over the life cycle (Table 44). Although the annual dollar outlay remains fairly constant, utilities as a percentage of annual child costs declines over the life cycle.

Utility spending trends attributable to the presence of the second and third child average 13 and 10% respectively. Although a decreasing percentage of the second child's annual costs are spent on utilities, an increasing percentage of the third child's annual costs are allocated to utilities, especially during the teen years.

Health Care

Outlays for health care comprise the smallest portion for first, second and third child of average annual child rearing costs. It includes money spent for eye glasses or eye care, pharmaceutical products, dental care (orthodontics, etc.), and health insurance premiums. (See Appendix B for detailed expenditure accounts.)

In 1982, for a monthly premium of $56.70, the province of Ontario provided coverage for routine health care that included routine eye exams carried out by an optometrist. No preventative dental care coverage was included.

Expenditures for first, second, and third child's health care average about 3, 2, and 1%, respectively of their total child rearing costs over the life cycle (Table 44). As a percentage of annual costs, health care expenditures peak around 13 years of age and decline thereafter.

Household Operations

For each child, household operation constitutes the second to the smallest portion of child rearing costs. It includes outlays for household cleaning supplies, pet supplies, household and clothing textiles, services related to furnishings and clothing plus personal care supplies and services. (See Appendix B for detailed expenditure accounts.)

Expenditures for household operations average 7, 3 and 2% of the first, second, and third child's total cost over the life cycle (Table 44). Increased expenditures due to the presence of the second and third child emerge as each reaches ages seven and ten respectively and steadily increase while siblings are present in the household.

HOUSING

As mentioned in the introduction, none of the previously discussed child cost estimates include an allowance for housing costs. It is being treated as a separate budget item similar to court cases where child support and matrimonial property awards are concurrently determined. Of particular interest are those instances where a matrimonial home is included in jointly held matrimonial property. Although in most situations the custodial parent is allowed to remain in the home, final ownership of the property may be retained by either or both parents, depending on the outcome of mediation. In circumstances where the custodial parent is also owner of the property, side deals for fair compensation of housing costs attributable to the child may be necessary.

For these reasons, we examine housing costs apart from other child rearing costs. Further, because court child support awards differentially compensate custodial parents who rent their residence from those who share in ownership of a matrimonial home, and because analysis has revealed that renters incur different costs than owners, we will discuss each separately.

Owned Housing

Our measure of owned housing costs represents a departure from its traditional treatment in the literature. Most researchers who have used consumer expenditure data to examine family budgeting adopt the definition of owned housing expenditures used by the data collection agency. For example, Statistics Canada includes outlays for maintenance and repairs, property tax, insurance and mortgage interest in its housing definition. Most notably excluded from this definition are mortgage principal payments. While in a strict accounting sense these payments actually represent a net change in assets, for purposes of planning for meeting child rearing costs, most families require access to annual estimates of how much money they need to set aside to meet the increased demand for housing necessitated by the child's presence, regardless of whether that allocation goes to mortgage interest or principal. Thus, the academic distinction between mortgage interest and principal is less important than providing families in varying circumstances with some idea of what they might actually spend for total housing.

Our definition of owned housing expenditures includes all of the traditionally defined components as well as payments to mortgage principal. This approach is not intended to diminish the important role of owned housing equity accrual as a financial planning tool, but rather emphasizes the need to develop alternative accounting measures appropriate to the purpose of the planning exercise, e.g., financial planning to meet child rearing costs versus retirement consumption needs.

Although we discuss the independent influence of children on housing expenditures of home owners and renters, in fact, the presence of children in Ontario households significantly influences the probability of home ownership. For example, the addition of a child (the first) to the family increases the probability of home ownership by about 22%.[3]

Table 45 presents information about the percentage of gross income that Ontario home owners spend for housing. Overall, the percentage of income allocated to owned housing decreases with family size. This does not necessarily imply that families with more children have homes of the same or lower values as their counterparts with fewer children, but that they reallocate their resources, perhaps by financing their mortgage over a longer period, such that their monthly housing outlay is equivalent or less.

It is reasonable to assume that families move into larger and more expensive living accommodations as the result of the presence of children. To estimate the amount of money families can plan on paying for this additional space, we examined the average cost per room paid by Ontario home owners. On average, the addition of a room necessitates an increase in housing expenditures by about 15% or about 2% of gross income. For simplicity, we will assume that each child will require additional space the equivalent of one room. *Thus, for home owners, 2% per child should be added to annual child rearing costs to cover increased housing requirements necessitated by the child's presence.*

Rental Housing

Table 45 also presents data regarding the percentages of income that Ontario renters of different family types allocate to housing. The percentage of income allocated to housing is relatively invariant to family size. This seemingly anomalous result has been found in previous studies and explained by the fact that large rental housing is not readily available. Thus as family size increases, families who continue to rent are less able to move to a larger, and thus more costly, unit.

An important distinction between expenditures by renters versus owners is not only that over time owners are accumulating assets, but also that owners pay a smaller and smaller share of gross income to meet housing costs, as their fixed mortgage payment composes a smaller and smaller share of annual income. Renters, on the other hand, face allocating a relatively constant share of income to housing over the life cycle as rental payments increase, keeping pace with increases in the overall cost-of-living index.

Our data indicate that Ontario renters spend about 10% more on housing (or 2% of annual gross income) by increasing their house or apartment size by one room. *Thus, for renters, 2% per child should be added to annual child rearing costs to cover increased housing requirements due to the child's presence.*

CHILD CARE

Child care expenses are a second category of expenditures that we have identified to study apart from other child rearing costs. There are differences in expenditures across family types depending on whether one or both parents are employed in the labour force. Our definition of child care expenditures includes outlays for babysitting and child care, both in and outside the home, as long as money was not paid to an immediate household member.

Table 46 presents information on the percentage of gross income that various sizes of families spend on child care according to whether one or both parents are employed outside the home. Over an 11-year period, families with two children where both parents are employed, spend about 3% of gross income for day care. One-, two-, and three-child families where only one parent is employed spend less than 1% of gross income for child care.

TOTAL CHILD REARING COSTS

Table 47 presents a summary of total child rearing costs as a percentage of gross income for families who own their own home and where both parents are employed in the labour force. On average, families with one child spend about 15% of their gross income to meet child rearing costs, two-child families about 24% and three-child families about 32%. Small economies to scale are noted for the second child, and for the third child. Since renters pay about the same for housing on a per room basis, their average costs, including day care if both parents are employed, would be similar to that of home owners.

OTHER DURABLE GOODS

Our analysis has excluded outlays for durable goods that may be attributable to the presence of children. Omitted are expenditures for recreational vehicles, boats, new and used automobiles, household furnishings and appliances. This is a departure from previous studies that included all the above in various expenditure categories. In a previous study, the authors found that about 9% of an average Canadian family's expenditures could be classified as going toward the purchase of durable goods, 5% of which is attributable to vehicle purchase. While childless couples appeared to allocate a fairly constant share of total expenditures for durable goods over the life cycle, peaks in the budget shares two-child families allocated to durable goods occurred in each year that a child was born, and at the stage in the life cycle where children reached driving age. One can easily speculate on the nature of spending behaviour that would cause these differences.

Again, since previous studies of child rearing costs included durable outlays in their expenditure definitions, our child rearing costs will be less than theirs. To the extent durable purchases are made for the benefit of children and that the assets are depreciated by the child's use, our estimates will underestimate the costs of children. More technically stated, if due to depreciation attributable to the child's use, net asset accrual is less than what it would have been had the child not benefitted from or used the durable goods, our estimates will understate the cost of raising children.

MEETING CHILD REARING COSTS

Seldom is the arrival of a child accompanied by an increase in income sufficient to meet the additional demands placed on family resources. Families meet these demands in several ways. First, they may increase the amount of time spent in the labour force. This strategy is more common during the later stages of the life cycle when the child's needs are less time and more goods intensive. During the early stages of the life cycle, however, it is more common that family income decreases as parents choose to meet the demands of child rearing by increasing the amount of time spent working in the home.

Another strategy used by parents to meet child rearing costs is to reduce certain expenditures as compared to what they would have spent had a child not been present in the household. Ontario families tend to spend less for food eaten away from home, recreation, adult goods such as tobacco and alcohol, parental clothing, and gifts in order to meet child rearing costs.

Finally, families may choose to meet the costs of child rearing by saving less, that is, foregoing future consumption. Table 48 presents information regarding the savings patterns of various families. Change in savings includes not only contributions to conventional measures such as cash held in banks, contributions to Registered Retirement Savings Plans (RRSPs) and other financial assets, but also allocations towards the purchase of durable goods such as vehicles, recreational equipment, furniture, and appliances.

On average, families with children save less than their childless counterparts. Childless couples on average save 29% of gross income and tend to steadily increase their savings rates over the life cycle, while couples with one, two, and three children save about 22, 17, and 17% respectively and experience both upward and downward savings trends over similar stages of the life cycle.

END NOTES

1. Over an 18-, 20- and 22- year life cycle, respectively.
2. Throughout the text, when reference is made to families with more than one child, the implicit assumption is that children are spaced two years apart.
3. These estimates were derived by calculating marginal effects from probit regressions on a dichotomous dependent variable indicating whether or not the family owned their own home.

CHAPTER 6

CHILD REARING COSTS: QUEBEC

This chapter presents information on child rearing costs and how Quebec middle-income families manage their resources to meet those costs. On average over the life cycle, two-child families spend about 15% of gross income to meet child rearing costs. This does not include additional spending for child care, housing, or durable goods, such as vehicles, household furniture, appliances, and recreational equipment necessitated by the addition of children to the family. The addition of a child to Quebec families causes increases in expenditures for food at home, clothing, utilities, transportation, and education.

Families meet the cost of raising children in many ways, including increasing their incomes, increasing the amount of time spent in household work, reallocating income from other expenditures to child goods, or decreasing their savings. We examine the latter two strategies in this study. First, we find that Quebec families spend less for food away from home, household operation, recreation, adult goods such as tobacco and alcohol, parental clothing, and gifts in order to meet child rearing costs. Second, Quebec families with children also save less than their childless counterparts. Families with two children save about 22% of gross income during the child rearing years, compared to an average savings rate of 25% by childless couples over the same period.

The remainder of the chapter presents more detailed information and examples regarding Quebec child cost estimates. Immediately following are summary and itemized cost estimates by expenditure category over the life cycle. Housing and child care estimates are considered apart from other expenditures as they are often given special treatment in financial planning and court-awarded child support orders. We conclude with a discussion of how Quebec families reduce their savings in order to meet child rearing costs. The data tables described in the following sections are found in Part II. Similar data for upper-middle income Quebec families is in Tables 55-60 in Part II, while data for lower-middle income families is in Tables 67-72 also in Part II.

EXPENDITURE ESTIMATES

Table 61 reports percentages of gross annual income allocated to meeting child costs, *excluding* housing, durable goods, and child care. On average, over the life cycle, the marginal cost of the first, second, and third child is about 7, 9, and 10% of gross income. Over the life cycle, this amounts to an average of about 7, 15, and 22% of gross income[1] for one-, two-, and three-child families respectively. By excluding major durable items like housing and appliances from the cost estimates, we find no overall economies of scale present. Absolute dollar expenditures steadily increase as children age, reflecting the fact that, during the later stages of the life cycle, meeting children's physical requirements demands less household work time and more material goods. Not only do total outlays on behalf of children increase, but the allocation of child rearing costs among specific spending categories also varies over the life cycle.[2] The next sections summarize these trends.

Food at Home

Table 62 presents information on the percentages of annual child rearing costs allocated to specific spending categories for each child. Food at home comprises the largest portion of child rearing costs in every year of the life cycle. It consists of food purchased from stores, and does *not* include food purchased in restaurants and fast food outlets. (See Appendix B for detailed expenditure accounts.)

Expenditures for food at home for an only child average 68% of total child rearing costs over the life cycle (Table 62). Although expenditures for food at home first increase and then decrease as a percentage of total annual child costs over time, the absolute dollar outlays increase steadily. This trend simply reflects the fact that child costs increase at an annual rate greater than spending for food at home during the teen years.

For example, when the first child is five years of age, 69% of her total cost that year is composed of food costs. If family income equals $20,000 in that year, total child costs would amount to about $1,400 (7% annual cost (from Table 61) times $20,000), and food costs would equal $966. By the child's sixteenth year, food costs constitute 64% of her annual cost; however, total costs since the fifth year have increased by 1% and income will have increased by approximately 24% (assuming 2%/year real income growth rate) such that annual food at home costs would be about $1,270 (8% annual cost (from Table 61) times a gross annual income of $24,800).

Food at home expenditures average 66 and 60% (Table 62) of the total costs for second and third children, respectively, over the life cycle.

As a percentage of annual costs, food at home increases over time, while siblings remain in the home.

Clothing

Clothing makes up the second largest portion of child rearing costs. It includes outlays for both children's clothing and adult clothing purchased for children age 13 and older. Expenditures for outerwear, accessories and footwear are also included in this category.

Expenditures for clothing for an only child average 11% of total child rearing costs over the life cycle (Table 62). Both the percentage of annual child costs and the absolute dollar outlay for clothing steadily increase over time. If, as in our previous example, annual child costs for one five-year-old child amount to 7% of gross income or $1,400, then clothing costs in that year amount to 14% (Table 62) of those costs, about $196.

Clothing expenditures for each of the second and third children average 15 and 24% respectively of their total child rearing costs over the life cycle. Although a larger portion of their costs are attributable to clothing expenditures, the percentage of second and third children's annual costs attributable to clothing, unlike the first child, decline over the life cycle while other siblings remain in the household.

Education and Related Expenditures

Education and related spending includes spending on tuition, lessons, school supplies, and reading materials such as books and magazine subscriptions. (See Appendix B for detailed expenditure accounts.)

Spending on education for a one-child family averages 5% of total costs (Table 62). Education as a percentage of total costs steadily increases as the child ages. No significant additional education expenditures are made for the second child until she is seven years of age. Because during the early years the two-child family allocates no additional funds to educational expenses (over what they would have spent had they only one child), the average expenditure as a percentage of the total cost over the life cycle is lower than that of the first child, at 3%.

Spending for the third child follows a pattern similar to that of the second child. No significant additional allocations to educational goods and services are made until the third child reaches age ten. Like the second child, educational expenditures as a percentage of total annual costs increase while other siblings are present in the household. Over the life cycle, approximately 2% of the third child's total cost is attributable to educational expenses.

Transportation

Transportation expenditures are comprised of spending for the operation of automobiles and trucks for personal use including fuel, maintenance and repairs, insurance and licence fees. Additional expenditures include outlays for bus, cab, trains, and plane fares. (See Appendix B for detailed expenditure accounts.) Expenditures on the purchase of vehicles are *not* included in transportation. Vehicle purchase is considered an investment and is part of savings (see discussion of Table 66).

Spending on transportation makes up 4% of the total cost of raising the first child (Table 62). Transportation expenditures, as a proportion of annual costs, are highest in the early and latter years of the life cycle. The proportion of annual costs allocated to transportation increases appreciably when the first child reaches driving age.

Transportation expenditures make up only a small part of the total costs of second and third children (Table 62). Spending on transportation as a percentage of the second and third child's costs occur as each nears driving age, and increases steadily. However, over the 18-year period, transportation expenditures compose only 2% of total child rearing costs for the second and third child.

Utilities

This category includes expenditures for water, heating fuel, electricity, and telephone. (See Appendix B for detailed expenditure accounts.) Expenditures for utilities attributable to the presence of an only child average 10% of total child rearing costs over the life cycle (Table 62). Although the annual dollar outlay remains fairly constant, utilities as a percentage of annual child costs declines over the life cycle.

Utility spending trends attributable to the presence of the second and third child average 7 and 6% respectively. Although a decreasing percentage of the second child's annual costs are spent on utilities, an increasing percentage of the third child's annual costs are allocated to utilities, especially in the teen years.

HOUSING

As mentioned in the introduction, none of the previously discussed child cost estimates include an allowance for housing costs. It is being treated as a separate budget item similar to court cases where child support and matrimonial property awards are concurrently determined. Of particular interest are those instances where a matrimonial home is included in jointly held matrimonial property.

Although in most situations the custodial parent is allowed to remain in the home, final ownership of the property may be retained by either or both parents, depending on the outcome of mediation. In circumstances where the custodial parent is also the owner of the property, side deals for fair compensation of housing costs attributable to the child may be needed.

For these reasons, we examine housing costs apart from other child rearing costs. Further, because court child support awards differentially compensate custodial parents who rent their residence from those who share in ownership of a matrimonial home, and because analysis has revealed that renters incur different costs than owners, we will discuss each separately.

Owned Housing

Our measure of owned housing costs represents a departure from its traditional treatment in the literature. Most researchers who have used consumer expenditure data to examine family budgeting adopt the definition of owned housing expenditures used by the data collection agency. For example, Statistics Canada includes outlays for maintenance and repairs, property tax, insurance and mortgage interest in its housing definition. Most notably excluded from this definition are mortgage principal payments. While in a strict accounting sense these payments actually represent a net change in assets, for purposes of planning for meeting child rearing costs, most families require access to annual estimates of how much money they need to set aside to meet the increased demand for housing necessitated by the child's presence, regardless of whether that allocation goes to mortgage interest or principal. Thus, the academic distinction between mortgage interest and principal is less important than providing families in varying circumstances with some idea of what they might actually spend for total housing.

Our definition of owned housing expenditures includes all of the traditionally defined components as well as payments to mortgage principal. This approach is not intended to diminish the important role of owned housing equity accrual as a financial planning tool, but rather emphasizes the need to develop alternative accounting measures appropriate to the purpose of the planning exercise, e.g., financial planning to meet child rearing costs versus retirement consumption needs.

Although we discuss the independent influence of children on housing expenditures of home owners and renters, in fact the presence of children in Quebec households significantly influences the probability of home ownership. For example, the addition of a child (the first) to the family increases the probability of home ownership by about 32%.[3]

Table 63 presents information about the percentage of gross income that Quebec home owners spend for housing. Overall the percentage of income allocated to housing does not vary significantly with family size. This does not necessarily imply that families with more children have homes of the same value as their counterparts with fewer children, but that they reallocate their resources, perhaps by financing their mortgage over a longer period, such that their monthly housing outlay is equivalent.

It is reasonable to assume that families move into larger and more expensive living accommodations as the result of the presence of children. To estimate the amount of money families can plan on paying for this additional space, we examined the average cost per room paid by Quebec home owners. On average, the addition of a room necessitates an increase in housing expenditures by about 10% or about 1% of gross income. For simplicity, we will assume that each child will require additional space the equivalent of one room. *Thus, for home owners, 1% per child should be added to annual child rearing costs to cover increased housing requirements necessitated by the child's presence.*

Rental Housing

Table 63 also presents data regarding the percentages of income that Quebec renters of different family types allocate to housing. Like home owners, the percentage of income allocated to housing is invariant to family size. This seemingly anomalous result has been found in previous studies and explained by the fact that large rental housing is not readily available. Thus as family size increases, families who continue to rent are less able to move to larger, more costly, units.

An important distinction between expenditures by renters versus owners is not only that over time owners are accumulating assets, but also that owners pay a smaller and smaller share of gross income to meet housing costs as their fixed mortgage payment composes a smaller and smaller share of annual income. Renters, on the other hand, face allocating a relatively constant share of income to housing over the life cycle as rental payments increase, keeping pace with increases in the overall cost-of-living index.

Our data indicate that Quebec renters spend about 15% more on housing (or 2% of annual gross income) by increasing their house or apartment size by one room. *Thus, for renters, 2% per child should be added to annual child rearing costs to cover increased housing requirements necessitated by the child's presence.*

CHILD CARE

Child care expenses are a second category of expenditures that we have identified to study apart from other child rearing costs. There are differences in expenditures across family types depending on whether one or both parents are employed in the labour force. Our definition of child care expenditures include outlays for babysitting and child care, both in and outside the home, as long as money was not paid to an immediate household member.

Table 64 presents information on the percentage of gross income that various sizes of families spend on child care according to whether one or both parents are employed outside the home. Over an 11-year period, families with two children where both parents are employed, spend about 2% of gross income for day care. One-, two-, and three-child families where only one parent is employed spend less than 1% for child care.

TOTAL CHILD REARING COSTS

Table 65 presents a summary of total child rearing costs as a percentage of gross income for families who own their own home and where both parents are employed in the labour force. On average, families with one child spend about 10% of their gross income to meet child rearing costs, two-child families about 19% and three-child families about 27%. Only small economies to scale are noted for the second and third child. Since renters pay about 1% per year more for housing, their average costs, including day care if both parents are employed, would be 1% higher.

OTHER DURABLE GOODS

Our analysis has excluded outlays for durable goods that may be attributable to the presence of children. Omitted are expenditures for recreational vehicles, boats, new and used automobiles, household furnishings and appliances. This is a departure from previous studies that included all the above in various expenditure categories. In a previous study, the authors found that about 9% of an average Canadian family's expenditures could be classified as going toward the purchase of durable goods, 5% of which is attributable to vehicle purchase. While childless couples appeared to allocate a fairly constant share of total expenditures for durable goods over the life cycle, peaks in the budget shares two-child families allocated to durable goods occurred in each year that a child was born, and at the stage in the life cycle where children reached driving age. One can easily speculate on the nature of spending behaviour that would cause these differences.

Again, since previous studies of child rearing costs included durable outlays in their expenditure definitions, our child rearing costs will be less than theirs. To the extent durable purchases are made for the benefit of children and that the assets are depreciated by the child's use, our estimates will underestimate the costs of children. More technically stated, if due to depreciation attributable to the child's use, net asset accrual is less than what it would have been had the child not benefitted from or used the durable goods, our estimates will understate the cost of raising children.

MEETING CHILD REARING COSTS

Seldom is the arrival of a child accompanied by an increase in income sufficient to meet the additional demands placed on family resources. Families meet these demands in several ways. First, they may increase the amount of time spent in the labour force. This strategy is more common during the later stages of the life cycle when the child's needs are less time, and more goods intensive. During the early stages of the life cycle, however, it is more common that family income decreases as parents choose to meet the demands of child rearing by increasing the amount of time spent working in the home.

Another strategy used by parents to meet child rearing costs is to reduce certain expenditures as compared to what they would have spent had a child not been present in the household. Quebec families tend to spend less for food eaten away from home, household operation, recreation, adult goods such as tobacco and alcohol, parental clothing, and gifts in order to meet child rearing costs.

Finally, families may choose to meet the costs of child rearing by saving less; that is, foregoing future consumption. Table 66 presents information regarding the savings patterns of various families. Change in savings includes not only contributions to conventional measures such as cash held in banks, contributions to Registered Retirement Savings Plans (RRSPs) and other financial assets, but also allocations towards the purchase of durable goods such as vehicles, recreational equipment, furniture, and appliances.

On average, families with children save less than their childless counterparts. Childless couples save an average of 25% of gross income and tend to steadily increase their savings rates over the life cycle, while couples with one, two, and three children save an average of 22% and experience both upward and downward savings trends over similar stages of the life cycle.

END NOTES

1. Over an 18-, 20- and 22- year life cycle, respectively.
2. Throughout the text, when reference is made to families with more than one child, the implicit assumption is that children are spaced two years apart.
3. These estimates were derived by calculating marginal effects from probit regressions on a dichotomous dependent variable indicating whether or not the family owned their own home.

CHAPTER 7

CHILD REARING COSTS: ATLANTIC REGION

This chapter presents information on child rearing costs and how Atlantic (Newfoundland, Nova Scotia, New Brunswick and Prince Edward Island), middle-income families manage their resources to meet those costs. On average over the life cycle, two-child families spend about 17% of gross income to meet child rearing costs. This does not include additional spending for child care, housing, or durable goods, such as vehicles, household furniture, appliances, and recreational equipment necessitated by the addition of children to the family. The addition of a child to Atlantic families causes increases in expenditures for food at home, clothing, utilities, transportation, education, and household operation.

Families meet the cost of raising children in many ways, including increasing their incomes, increasing the amount of time spent in household work, reallocating income from other expenditures to child goods, or decreasing their savings. We examine the latter two strategies in this study. First, we find that Atlantic families spend less for food away from home, recreation, adult goods such as tobacco and alcohol, parental clothing, and gifts in order to meet child rearing costs. Second, Atlantic families with children also save less than their childless counterparts. Families with two children save about 28% of gross income during the child rearing years compared to an average savings rate of 33% by childless couples over the same period.

The remainder of the chapter presents more detailed information and examples regarding Atlantic child cost estimates. Immediately following are summary and itemized cost estimates by expenditure category over the life cycle. Housing and child care estimates are considered apart from other expenditures as they are often given special treatment in financial planning and court-awarded child support orders. We conclude with a discussion of how Atlantic families reduce their savings in order to meet child rearing costs. The data tables described in the following sections are found in Part II. Similar data for upper-middle Atlantic families is found in Tables 73-78 in Part II, while data for lower-middle income families is in Tables 85-90 also in Part II.

EXPENDITURE ESTIMATES

Table 79 reports percentages of gross annual income allocated to meeting child costs, *excluding* housing, durable goods, and child care. On average, over the life cycle, the marginal cost of the first, second, and third child is about 9, 9, and 10% of gross income. Over the life cycle, this amounts to an average of 9, 17, and 23% of gross income[1] for one-, two-, and three-child families respectively. By excluding major durable items like housing and appliances from the cost estimates, we find no economies of scale present. Costs as a percentage of gross income increase as children age, reflecting the fact that, during the later stages of the life cycle, meeting children's physical requirements demands less household work time and more material goods. Not only do total outlays on behalf of children increase, but the allocation of child rearing costs among specific spending categories also varies over the life cycle.[2] The next sections summarize these trends.

Food at Home

Table 80 presents information on the percentages of annual child rearing costs allocated to specific spending categories for each child. Food at home comprises the largest portion of child rearing costs in every year of the life cycle. It consists of food purchased from stores, and does *not* include food purchased in restaurants and fast food outlets. (See Appendix B for detailed expenditure accounts.)

Expenditures for food at home for an only child average 55% of total child rearing costs over the life cycle (Table 80). Although expenditures for food at home first increase and then decrease as a percentage of total annual child costs over time, the absolute dollar outlays increase steadily. This trend simply reflects the fact that child costs increase at an annual rate greater than spending for food at home during the teen years.

For example, when the first child is five years of age, 61% of her total cost that year is composed of food costs. If family income equals $20,000 in that year, total child costs would amount to about $1,600 (8% annual cost (from Table 79) times $20,000), and food costs would equal $976. By the child's sixteenth year, food costs constitute only 45% of her annual cost; however, total costs since the fifth year have increased by 3% and income will have increased by approximately 24% (assuming 2%/year real income growth rate) such that annual food at home costs would be about $1,228 (11% annual cost (from Table 79) times a gross annual income of $24,800).

Food at home expenditures average 64 and 59% (Table 80) of the total costs for second and third children, respectively, over the life cycle.

As a percentage of annual costs, food at home increases then decreases over time, a trend similar to that of the one-child family.

Clothing

Clothing expenditures include outlays for both children's clothing and adult clothing purchased for children age 13 and older. Expenditures for outerwear, accessories and footwear are also included in this category.

Expenditures for clothing for an only child average 8% of total child rearing costs over the life cycle (Table 80). The percentage of annual child costs for clothing increase and then decrease over time. If, as in our previous example, annual child costs for one five-year-old child amount to 8% of gross income or $1,600, then clothing costs in that year amount to 13% (Table 80) of those costs, about $208.

Clothing expenditures for each of the second and third children average 18 and 28% respectively of their total child rearing costs over the life cycle. Although a larger portion of their costs are attributable to clothing expenditures than the first child, the percentage of second and third children's annual costs attributable to clothing, similarly decline over the life cycle while other siblings remain in the household.

Education and Related Expenditures

Education-related expenses include spending on tuition, lessons, school supplies, and reading materials such as books and magazine subscriptions. (See Appendix B for detailed expenditure accounts.)

Spending on education for a one-child family averages 6% of total child rearing costs (Table 80). Education as a percentage of total costs steadily increases as the child ages. No significant additional education expenditures are made for the second child until she is 12 years of age. Thereafter, educational spending for the second child follows an increasing trend. Because during the early years the two-child family allocates no additional funds to educational expenses (over what they would have spent had they only one child), the average expenditure as a percentage of the total cost over the life cycle is lower than that of the first child, at 3%.

Spending for the third child follows a pattern similar to that of the second child. No significant additional allocations to educational goods and services are made until the third child reaches age 14. Over the life cycle, approximately 2% of the third child's total cost is attributable to educational expenses.

Transportation

Transportation expenditures are comprised of spending for the operation of automobiles and trucks for personal use, including fuel, maintenance and repairs, insurance and licence fees. Additional expenditures include outlays for bus, cab, trains, and plane fares. (See Appendix B for detailed expenditure accounts.) Expenditures on the purchase of vehicles are *not* included in transportation. Vehicle purchase is considered to be an investment and is included in savings (see discussion of Table 84).

Spending on transportation composes 10% of the total cost of raising the first child (Table 80). Transportation expenditures, as a proportion of annual costs, steadily increase over the life cycle.

Transportation expenditures constitute only a small part of the total costs of second and third children (Table 80). Spending on transportation as a percentage of the second and third child's costs occurs as each nears driving age and increase steadily. However, over the 18-year period, transportation expenditures compose only 4% of total child rearing costs for the second and third child.

Utilities

Utility-related expenses include expenditures for water, heating fuel, electricity, and telephone. (See Appendix B for detailed expenditure accounts.)

Expenditures for utilities attributable to the presence of an only child average 8% of total child rearing costs over the life cycle (Table 80). Although the annual dollar outlay remains fairly constant, utilities as a percentage of annual child costs declines over the life cycle.

Utility spending trends attributable to the presence of the second and third child average 5 and 3% respectively. A decreasing percentage of the second child's annual costs over the life cycle are spent on utilities, while additional expenditures due to the third child are only incurred during the early and teen years of the life cycle.

Household Operations

Household operation makes up 12% of the child rearing costs for one child. For the second and third child, household operation makes up a small portion of child rearing costs. It includes outlays for household cleaning supplies, pet supplies, household and clothing textiles, services related to furnishings and clothing plus personal care supplies and services. (See Appendix B for detailed expenditure accounts.) Expenditures for household operations average 12, 5 and 3% of the first, second, and third child's total cost over the life cycle (Table 80).

HOUSING

As mentioned in the introduction, none of the previously discussed child cost estimates include an allowance for housing costs. It is being treated as a separate budget item similar to court cases where child support and matrimonial property awards are concurrently determined. Of particular interest are those instances where a matrimonial home is included in jointly held matrimonial property. Although in most situations the custodial parent is allowed to remain in the home, final ownership of the property may be retained by either or both parents, depending on the outcome of mediation. In circumstances where the custodial parent is also owner of the property, side deals for fair compensation of housing costs attributable to the child may be necessary.

For these reasons, we examine housing costs apart from other child rearing costs. Further, because court child support awards differentially compensate custodial parents who rent their residence from those who share in ownership of a matrimonial home, and because analysis has revealed that renters incur different costs than owners, we will discuss each separately.

Owned Housing

Our measure of owned housing costs represents a departure from its traditional treatment in the literature. Most researchers who have used consumer expenditure data to examine family budgeting adopt the definition of owned housing expenditures used by the data collection agency. For example, Statistics Canada includes outlays for maintenance and repairs, property tax, insurance and mortgage interest in its housing definition. Most notably excluded from this definition are mortgage principal payments. While in a strict accounting sense, these payments actually represent a net change in assets, for purposes of planning for meeting child rearing costs, most families require access to annual estimates of how much money they need to set aside to meet the increased demand for housing necessitated by the child's presence, regardless of whether that allocation goes to mortgage interest or principal. Thus, the academic distinction between mortgage interest and principal is less important than providing families in varying circumstances with some idea of what they might actually spend for total housing.

Our definition of owned housing expenditures includes all of the traditionally defined components as well as payments to mortgage principal. This approach is not intended to diminish the important role of owned housing equity accrual as a financial planning tool, but rather emphasizes the need to develop alternative accounting measures appropriate to the purpose of the planning exercise, e.g., financial planning to meet child rearing costs versus retirement consumption needs.

Although we discuss the independent influence of children on housing expenditures of home owners and renters, in fact, the presence of children in Atlantic households significantly influences the probability of home ownership. For example, the addition of a child (the first) to the family increases the probability of home ownership by about 24%.[3]

Table 81 presents information about the percentage of gross income that Atlantic home owners spend for housing. Overall the percentage of income allocated to housing declines with family size. This does not necessarily imply that families with more children have homes of the same value as their counterparts with fewer children, but that they reallocate their resources, perhaps by financing their mortgage over a longer period, such that their monthly housing outlay is equivalent.

It is reasonable to assume that families move into larger and more expensive living accommodations as the result of the presence of children. To estimate the amount of money families can plan on paying for this additional space, we examined the average cost per room paid by Atlantic home owners. On average, the addition of a room necessitates an increase in housing expenditures by about 23% or about 2% of gross income. For simplicity, we will assume that each child will require additional space the equivalent of one room. *Thus, for home owners, 2% per child should be added to annual child rearing costs to cover increased housing requirements necessitated by the child's presence.*

Rental Housing

Table 81 also presents data regarding the percentages of income that Atlantic renters of different family types allocate to housing. Like home owners, the percentage of income allocated to housing declines with family size. This seemingly anomalous result has been found in previous studies and explained by the fact that large rental housing is not readily available. Thus, as family size increases, families who continue to rent are less able to move to a larger, and thus more costly, unit.

An important distinction between expenditures by renters versus owners is not only that, over time, owners are accumulating assets, but also that owners pay a smaller and smaller share of gross income to meet housing costs as their fixed mortgage payment makes up a smaller and smaller share of annual income. Renters, on the other hand, face allocating a relatively constant share of income to housing over the life cycle as rental payments increase, keeping pace with increases in the overall cost-of-living index.

Our data indicate that Atlantic renters spend about 8% more on housing (or 1% of annual gross income) by increasing their house or apartment size by one room. *Thus, for renters, 1% per child should be added to annual child rearing costs to cover increased housing requirements necessitated by the child's presence.*

CHILD CARE

Child care expenses are a second category of expenditures that we have identified to study apart from other child rearing costs. There are differences in expenditures across family types depending on whether one or both parents are employed in the labour force. Our definition of child care expenditures include outlays for babysitting and child care, both in and outside the home, as long as money was not paid to an immediate household member.

Table 82 presents information on the percentage of gross income that various sizes of families spend on child care according to whether one or both parents are employed outside the home. Over an 11-year period, families with one child, where both parents are employed, spend about 4% of gross income for day care. One-, two-, and three-child families where only one parent is employed spend less than 1% for child care.

TOTAL CHILD REARING COSTS

Table 83 presents a summary of total child rearing costs as a percentage of gross income for families who own their own home and where both parents are employed in the labour force. On average, families with one child spend about 14% of their gross income to meet child rearing costs, two-child families about 21% and three-child families about 29%. No economies to scale are noted for the third child. Since renters pay about 1% per year less for housing, their average costs, including day care if both parents are employed, would be 1% lower.

OTHER DURABLE GOODS

Our analysis has excluded outlays for durable goods that may be attributable to the presence of children. Omitted are expenditures for recreational vehicles, boats, new and used automobiles, household furnishings and appliances. This is a departure from previous studies that included all the above in various expenditure categories. In a previous study, the authors found that about 9% of an average Canadian family's expenditures could be classified as going toward the purchase of durable goods, 5% of which is attributable to vehicle purchase. While childless couples appeared to allocate a fairly constant share of total expenditures for durable goods over the life cycle, peaks in the budget shares two-child families allocated to durable goods, occurred in each year that a child was born, and at the stage in the life cycle where children reached driving age. One can easily speculate on the nature of spending behaviour that would cause these differences.

Again, since previous studies of child rearing costs included durable outlays in their expenditure definitions, our child rearing costs will be less than theirs. To the extent durable purchases are made for the benefit of children, and that the assets are depreciated by the child's use, our estimates will underestimate the costs of children. More technically stated, if due to depreciation attributable to the child's use, net asset accrual is less than what it would have been had the child not benefitted from or used the durable goods, our estimates will understate the cost of raising children.

MEETING CHILD REARING COSTS

Seldom is the arrival of a child accompanied by an increase in income sufficient to meet the additional demands placed on family resources. Families meet these demands in several ways. First, they may increase the amount of time spent in the labour force. This strategy is more common during the later stages of the life cycle when the child's needs are less time, and more goods intensive. During the early stages of the life cycle, however, it is more common that family income decreases as parents choose to meet the demands of child rearing by increasing the amount of time spent working in the home.

Another strategy used by parents to meet child rearing costs is to reduce certain expenditures as compared to what they would have spent had a child not been present in the household. Atlantic families tend to spend less for food eaten away from home, recreation, adult goods such as tobacco and alcohol, parental clothing, and gifts in order to meet child rearing costs.

Finally, families may choose to meet the costs of child rearing by saving less; that is, foregoing future consumption. Table 84 presents information regarding the savings patterns of various families. Change in savings includes not only contributions to conventional measures such as cash held in banks, contributions to Registered Retirement Savings Plans (RRSPs) and other financial assets, but also allocations towards the purchase of durable goods such as vehicles, recreational equipment, furniture, and appliances.

On average, families with children save less (28% of gross income) than their childless counterparts (33% of gross income). Childless couples tend to steadily increase their savings rates over the life cycle, while couples with children experience both upward and downward savings trends over similar stages of the life cycle.

END NOTES

1. Over an 18-, 20- and 22- year life cycle, respectively.
2. Throughout the text, when reference is made to families with more than one child, the implicit assumption is that children are spaced two years apart.
3. These estimates were derived by calculating marginal effects from probit regressions on a dichotomous dependent variable indicating whether or not the family owned their own home.

CHAPTER 8

REGIONAL OVERVIEW

Considering Canada's geographical diversity, one might expect substantial differences in family spending patterns by region. It is somewhat surprising, therefore, to note that much of our analysis reveals only minor regional differences. This result may be explained in part by two factors. First, our sample is a specific one: two-parent families, with and without children, not welfare dependent, below retirement age, with all members present the entire year. We have removed many of the possibilities for regional disparity by selecting this particular group. The second factor that may explain so few regional differences is the expression of the results in terms of percentages, rather than in actual dollar costs. The percentages of income spent on various commodities vary less by region than do the dollar amounts. The implications of using this methodology are discussed in Chapter 2.

The percentages of income spent on children by middle-income families, excluding housing, day care, and durable goods, are found in Part II – Table 7 for British Columbia, Table 25 for the Prairies, Table 43 for Ontario, Table 61 for Quebec, and Table 79 for the Atlantic. The average of this proportion over the life cycle varies from a low of 7% for the first child in Quebec (Table 61) to 11% for the first child in Ontario (Table 43). These tables show few economies to scale in raising children. That is, when housing, day care, and durable goods are not included, similar amounts are spent on the second child as on the first child. This result contradicts the popular notion that subsequent children are "cheaper" than the first, and in part may be explained by the exclusion of housing and durable goods from the analysis. Indeed, this seems to be the case, since the addition of housing and day care to the cost estimates reveals economies of scale for second and third children. [See Tables 11 (British Columbia), 29 (Prairies), 47 (Ontario), 65 (Quebec), and 83 (Atlantic) in Part II.] Including housing and day care does not substantially change the ranking of costs: Quebec families still show the lowest average proportion of income spent on children, 10% for the first child (Table 65), and Ontario the highest at 15% for the first child (Table 47).

Some of the variation in costs between regions is caused by differences in the prices of goods and services; families which face higher prices will spend a greater proportion of income on children. Ontario's higher percentages may reflect this region's higher prices. The higher costs may also be explained by the higher labour force participation rates of married women in this region. In 1982, 55.8% of married women in Ontario were employed in paid work outside the home,[1] the highest regional rate in the country. This suggests that Ontario families are more likely to substitute market goods and services for parental time in child rearing, which would increase the proportion of income spent on children. Other differences among regions which may affect the proportion of income allocated to children include the variation in the socialization of health care, and possible differences in cultural norms pertaining to raising children.

There are regional differences in the strategies which families use to meet child rearing costs. As has been stated in the introduction to each region in Chapters 3 to 7, families meet the cost of raising children in many ways, including increasing their incomes, increasing the amount of time spent in household work, reallocating income from other expenditures to child goods, or decreasing their savings. In all regions, families reallocated out of current income to meet child rearing costs. Families with children spent less on food away from home, tobacco and alcohol, parental clothing, and recreation than families without children in all regions.

Another strategy used by families to meet child rearing costs is to defer savings. Families in all regions saved less than their childless counterparts, but regional differences exist to the extent that this strategy is used. Families with one child living in Quebec, British Columbia and the Prairie regions saved 2-3% less than similar couples without children. Families living in the Atlantic region reduced savings an average of 5% in response to the presence of a child, while Ontario families lowered savings by an average of 7%. Savings includes not only conventional forms, such as savings accounts and bonds, but also purchases of durable goods, such as furniture, appliances, and recreational vehicles. Ontario families rely more on the reduction of savings than families in other regions. This suggests that families in regions other than Ontario may use methods of meeting child rearing costs, like increasing incomes or increasing time spent in household work, more often than do Ontario families.

END NOTE

1. Statistics Canada. *Labour Force Annual Averages 1981-1988*. Cat. # 71529.

CHAPTER 9

CALCULATING CHILD SUPPORT: CASE STUDIES

USING CHILD COST FIGURES AND WORK SHEETS

This chapter applies the figures presented in the regional analyses to the calculation of child rearing costs for establishing child maintenance awards. Following a discussion of when and how to use the information from the regional chapters, two case studies, each using a different region and different circumstances, are presented.

A basic premise often applied in setting child maintenance is that children should not be economically disadvantaged by the actions of their parents. In other words, children, post-separation, are entitled to remain close to their pre-separation standard of living. Thus, rather than ascertain the minimum amount of support required to meet children's basic needs, we adopt the principle of income sharing. Chapters 3 to 7 presented information on the proportion of income that families allocate to, or share with, their children. In this chapter, we apply those estimates to the income of the absent parent and assume the custodial parent would continue to contribute that proportion of her/his income that was allocated to children before separation.

Figures 9.1 and 9.2 show work sheets that can be used to calculate child maintenance. Figure 9.1 demonstrates how to compute the total proportion of gross income spent on children. The following section outlines step-by-step instructions on completing each of the work sheets.

Completing Figure 9.1 (page 71)

Step 1: The Year - Column A

The "year" column in Figure 9.1 refers to the chronological year and begins with the year of separation or the year that one wants to begin estimating child rearing costs. The last year given is the year that the youngest child becomes 18 years of age.

Step 2: The Ages of Children - Columns B, D, and F

For the year of separation, enter the age of each child as of December 31. Next, enter the children's ages at December 31 of the subsequent years, concluding each column when the child in question reaches age 18, the age of majority. Additional columns are given for second and third children if needed.[1]

Step 3: The Cost of Each Child - Columns C, E, and G

The percentages of income spent on first, second and third children are taken directly from the regional tables in Part II. Table 9.1 refers readers to the appropriate regional and income level figures.

In the year that each child turns 18, costs are included for that child only until her/his eighteenth birthday. The computation is as follows: first, calculate the number of days of the year between January 1 and the child's birthday and divide by 365; then, multiply that proportion by the annual per cent cost from the table. For example, 11% of gross income is spent on an 18-year-old child in a middle income family in British Columbia (Table 7). If this child's birthday were March 13, maintenance would only be paid in that year from January 1 to March 13. This period is 20% of the year (72/365). Thus, the proportion of income entered for this child in his/her eighteenth year is 2% (20% of 11%).

TABLE 9.1

GUIDE TO TABLES IN PART II WHICH LIST TOTAL CHILD COST, EXCLUDING HOUSING AND CHILD CARE, BY INCOME LEVEL

	Gross income level of absent parent:		
	Lower-middle ($15,000-30,000)	Middle ($30,000-45,000)	Upper-middle ($45,000-100,000)
British Columbia	Table 13	Table 7	Table 1
Prairies	Table 31	Table 25	Table 19
Ontario	Table 49	Table 43	Table 37
Quebec	Table 67	Table 61	Table 55
Atlantic	Table 85	Table 79	Table 73

Step 4: Child Care Costs - Column H

Families whose child care arrangements will not change after separation may wish to estimate their own expenditures. In this case, their child care estimates, expressed as a percentage of gross pre-separation family income, i.e., total annual family income prior to separation, should be entered in Column H. Conventionally, child care expenditures are expected to be zero when the child reaches age 12. Families uncertain of future child care costs can estimate these using the percentages from tables in the regional analysis chapters.[2] That information is presented by employment status of parents – one parent employed and two parents employed. If the custodial parent is employed, the figures for two parents should be used since these estimates were derived by examining expenditures of families without a full time homemaker.

Step 5: Housing Costs - Column I

Step 5a: Renters (Owners - see 5b)

In cases where families rent their dwelling, housing is part of the costs of children. Analyses of income allocated for an additional room in a rented unit are presented in the housing discussion of each regional chapter. [3] These figures are entered in Column I. For example, Quebec middle-income families pay 2% of gross income for an additional room in a rented unit. Thus, if there were one child present, 2% would be entered in Column I for each year of the analysis. If there were two children, the amount included in Column I would depend on the gender of the children and the difference in their ages. In our examples, we assume that one extra room is allocated for each child.

Step 5b: Owners (Renters - see 5a)

Owned housing is considered matrimonial property and is usually separate from child support awards. In most cases where the custodial parent remains in the family home, no additional consideration of the child's influence on housing costs is necessary; Column I is then left blank. See Chapters 3 to 7 for a discussion of the influence of children on owned housing.

Step 6: The Total Cost of Children - Column J

Summing the cost of each child (Columns C, E, and G) across for each year and the allocations for child care and housing (Columns H and I) yields annual total percentages of income spent on children which are used in Figure 9.2 (Column D).

In the year of separation, costs are included from the date of separation until the end of that year. To calculate the cost of children in the year of separation, first calculate the percentage that would be paid for the whole year. Then, calculate what proportion of the year child support is to be paid. For example if the date of separation were December 1, then 8% (31/365) of the year requires maintenance payment. Next, multiply the proportion of the year by the child cost computed for the full year. If the full year calculation in the December 1 separation is 10% then the total cost would be 1% (8% of 10%).

Completing Figure 9.2 (page 72)

Figure 9.2 shows the calculation of child costs for maintenance awards and yields actual dollar amounts.

Step 1: Absent Parent's Income in Year of Separation - Item A

This figure is the gross income of the absent parent in the year of separation. It is used in Column C to estimate real incomes in subsequent years.

Step 2: The Year - Column B

The "year" column in Figure 9.2 is identical to Column A in Figure 9.1 and refers to the chronological year. The first year entered is the year of separation and the last one entered is the year that the youngest child turns 18 years of age.

Step 3: Projecting Income - Column C

Our estimates of child costs are based on the assumption that incomes increase over time. In part, this increase in income explains the relatively constant child cost estimates as percentages of income over the life cycle we found: if we assumed a constant income stream, the percentage of income spent on children over the life cycle would increase more quickly.

Studies of long term income trends reveal that, over time, real incomes on average increase by 2% annually. Estimating incomes for each year of child support allows for normal income growth, which the children would share. Maintenance awards that are set at a specific dollar amount and not changed from year to year decrease the costs as a percentage of income and do not take income changes into account.

The figures to calculate a 2% annual increase in income are included in the work sheet. To compute projected income, multiply A by the factor given for each year.

Step 4: Cost of Children - Column D

Enter the percentages calculated in Figure 9.1 - Column J.

Step 5: Annual Child Maintenance - Column E

Annual child maintenance is computed by multiplying Column C, projected income, by Column D, to get an annual dollar amount for child maintenance. All figures are expressed in terms of the dollar values of the year of separation, which means that actual dollar amounts spent in subsequent years will be higher because of inflation.

The reader is again reminded that estimates used in Figures 9.1 and 9.2 do not include any allowance for the influence of the presence of children on the purchase of durable goods, such as vehicles, household furniture and appliances.

CASE STUDY EXAMPLES

The following two cases illustrate the use of Figures 9.1 and 9.2 under differing circumstances.

Case I: The Cost of Raising an Only Child in British Columbia

Case Specifics

Bruce and Claire Johnson were married for five years and were separated on April 18, 1988. There is one child from the marriage, Jerilyn, born September 21, 1986. Bruce and Claire have agreed that Bruce will be the primary care giver for Jerilyn and that Claire will pay child support. Bruce and Jerilyn continue to rent the two bedroom apartment in Vancouver that Bruce and Claire had lived in prior to their separation. Bruce, age 30, teaches high school and has an annual gross income of $31,000. Claire, 25, is a paramedic with an ambulance service whose salary for this year is $26,000. Jerilyn has been in full time child care for a year, which costs the Johnsons $190 a month.

Calculating the Maintenance Award

The calculation of the amount that Claire will contribute to Jerilyn's maintenance involves computing the percentage of her income that she would have spent on Jerilyn's upbringing had the separation not occurred and were she the sole economic supporter. Claire's contribution does not constitute the total cost of raising Jerilyn: Bruce, as custodial parent, is also assumed to contribute the same fraction of his income to Jerilyn's upbringing. The completed work sheets for the Johnson case are shown in Figures 9.3 and 9.4.

Completing Figure 9.3 for the Johnsons (page 73)

Step 1: Year - Column A

The year of separation, 1988, is entered as the first year. The period of time for which child support is required has to be computed. In this case Claire will be paying maintenance until 2004, when Jerilyn reaches age 18.

Step 2: Age of First Child - Column B

The first line of this column contains Jerilyn's age at the end of the year of separation. The remainder of the column contains her age at the end of each corresponding year and ends when she is 18.

Step 3: Cost of First Child - Column C

This column uses information on average percentages of income spent on the first child in British Columbia. Claire's $26,000 salary places her in the lower-middle income category. Table 13 contains the per cent of income spent on children by lower-middle income British Columbia families. The figures for the first child in Table 13 are entered in Column C, beginning with the number for the child at age 2. As there is only one child, Columns D-G in Figure 9.3 are left blank.

Step 4: Child Care - Column H

Jerilyn's child care costs total $2,280 annually. This amount is 4% of the Johnson's gross income before separation. Since the actual proportion of gross income spent on child care is known, this figure can be used for Column H instead of the averages presented in the regional chapters. Note that the 4% of income Claire pays is not the total cost of child care; 4% of $26,000 is $1,040, and represents the proportion of the costs that she would have paid if no separation had occurred. The Johnsons do not know how much they will need to pay for child care once Jerilyn is school age. For the years when Jerilyn is age 6-11, averages for lower-middle income British Columbia families (Table 16) are used as the proportion of income Claire pays for child care (Column H).

Step 5: Housing - Column I

Column I of Figure 9.3 shows housing costs allocated to Jerilyn. Since the Johnsons are renters, there is no matrimonial home subject to division. Data for lower-middle income renters in British Columbia indicates that 1% of gross income is spent for each additional room (see note on Table 17). Thus 1% is given in Column I as Claire's share of the cost of renting an additional room for Jerilyn.

Step 6: Total Cost - Column J

Column J represents the totals for Columns C, H and I for each year. The cost in the year of separation, 1988, is calculated first for the entire year, which totals 12%. Then, the total is multiplied by the fraction of the year involved. April 18 - December 31 is 70% of the year (257/365), so the total shown in Figure 9.4 is 9% (70% of 12%). Maintenance is paid up to Jerilyn's eighteenth birthday. Thus, a partial year calculation has to be performed. The total percentage computed for Jerilyn's eighteenth year is 9%. The period from January 1 to September 21 (Jerilyn's birthday) is 72% of the whole year (265/366). The total percentage in the last year is then 6% (72% of 9%).

Completing Figure 9.4 for the Johnsons (page 74)

Step 1: Income of Absent Parent - Item A

Claire's income in the year of separation (1988) is $26,000. This figure is entered in A.

Step 2: Year - Column B

The year of separation is 1988, which is entered as the first year. The period of time for which child support is required has to be computed. In this case, Claire will be paying maintenance until 2004, for the years for which Jerilyn is 2 until age 18.

Step 3: Projected Income - Column C

The next step is to estimate Claire's income for the years 1989 to 2004. Her income in 1988 is $26,000. The figures needed to calculate the 2% annual increase (described above) are included in the work sheet.

Step 4: Cost of Children - Column D

These figures are taken from Column J of Figure 9.3.

Step 5: Annual Child Maintenance - Column E

Calculating the amount that Claire will allocate to Jerilyn's upbringing is then carried out by multiplying her annual projected income (Column C) by the fraction of income normally spent on children by lower-middle income British Columbia families when housing and child care are included (Column D). Maintenance is different each year, as Jerilyn ages and different costs are included, i.e., child care costs are only incurred until Jerilyn is age 11.

Case II: The Cost of Raising Two Children in Ontario

Case Specifics

Bill and Linda Olson have been married for 11 years. They have two children, Kelly, born October 6, 1980, and Kim, born February 17, 1984. When their first child was born, Linda quit her job as a nurse and worked as a full time homemaker. Bill is employed as an autoworker with an annual salary of $44,000. Since their separation August 3, 1988, Linda has continued to care for the two children full time, and to live with them in the couple's three bedroom bungalow in Oshawa.

Calculating the Maintenance Award

Figures 9.5 and 9.6 show the calculation of the amount of child support Bill will pay for the next 14 years.

Completing Figure 9.5 for the Olsons (page 75)

Step 1: Year - Column A

The year of separation is 1988, which is entered as the first year. The period of time for which child support is required has to be computed. In this case, Bill will be paying maintenance until 2002, when Kim reaches age 18.

Step 2: Age of First Child - Column B

Kelly's age at the end of 1988 (the year of separation) is 8 and is entered as the first year. The last age entered is age 18.

Step 3: Cost of First Child - Column C

Bill's $44,000 income falls within the middle-income category, so the first child's cost is taken from Table 43 for the ages 8-18. In Kelly's eighteenth year, 1998, support will be provided until her eighteenth birthday – October 6. The period from January 1 to October 6 is 76% of the year (279/365). The cost for the whole year is 15% (Table 43). Thus, the figure entered for Kelly's eighteenth year is 11% (76% of 15%).

Step 4: Age of Second Child - Column D

Kim's age at the end of 1988 is 4 and is entered as the first year. The last age entered is 18.

Step 5: Cost of Second Child - Column E

Costs for Kim are also taken from Table 43, the column corresponding to the second child. These are listed for the second child aged 4-18. In Kim's eighteenth year costs are paid from January 1 to February 17 (Kim's birthday). This period is 13% of the year. Table 43 shows the cost of the second child at age 18 is 14%. The figure entered here is 2% (13% of 14%).

As there is no third child in the Olson family, Columns F and G are left blank.

Step 6: Child Care - Column H

As the discussion outlining specific costs (Chapters 3 to 7) indicates, families with one earner spend very little on child care. The amount that the average Ontario family spends on child care is shown in Table 46. Families with one earner do not incur any appreciable amount of child care costs beyond the child's first year; thus, in the Olson case, no addition is made for child care. If, as a result of the separation, Linda returns to paid employment or to school, then child care expenses would be an important consideration. The percentages for two parents employed could then be included in Figure 9.5.

Step 7: Housing - Column I

Since the Olsons own their home, it is regarded as part of the matrimonial property to be divided between the spouses. Thus, considerations about housing expenditures on children's behalf become less germane to the child support award question. Therefore, no adjustment is made in the housing column.

Step 8: Total Cost of Children - Column J

Summing the cost of each child (Columns C and E) across for each year yields annual percentages of income spent on the two children which are used in Column D of Figure 9.6.

Completing Figure 9.6 for the Olsons (page 76)

Step 1: Income of the Absent Parent - Item A

Bill's gross income in the year of separation (1988) is $44,000.

Step 2: Year - Column B

The year column is the same as Column A in Figure 9.5. The first year is the year of separation, 1988, and the last is the year Kim turns 18, 2002.

Step 3: Projected Income - Column C

The next step is to estimate Bill's income for the years 1989 to 2002. His income in 1988 is $44,000. The figures needed to calculate the 2% annual increase (described above) are included in the work sheet.

Step 4: Cost of Children - Column D

The figures shown here are taken from Column J in Figure 9.5.

Step 5: Annual Child Maintenance - Column E

Calculation of the amount that Bill will allocate to Kelly and Kim's upbringing is then carried out by multiplying his annual projected income (Column C) by the percentage of income normally spent on children by two-child, middle-income, Ontario families when housing and child care are included. In this case, there are no adjustments for either housing or child care. The maintenance paid changes each year as the children age and income grows.

The amount paid in the year of separation, 1988, is calculated for the entire year first, which totals $7,480. Then, the total is multiplied by the fraction of the year involved. August 3 - December 31 is 41% of the year (150/365), so the total shown in Figure 9.6 is $3,067 (41% of $7,480).

END NOTES

1. No data are presented for families with more than three children. The cost of the fourth child is similar to the cost of the third child, and thus the estimates used for a third child could be used to approximate the cost of a fourth child. The data used here contained few families with more than four children, and thus should only cautiously be applied to larger families.
2. Tables 4, 10, 16 (British Columbia), 22, 28, 34 (Prairies), 40, 46, 52 (Ontario), 58, 64, 70 (Quebec), 76, 82, 88 (Atlantic) provide information on the proportion of income spent on daycare by employment status of parents for each income level.
3. This information can also be found in note b of the total child cost tables which include housing for each income level: Tables 5, 11, 17 (British Columbia); 23, 29, 35 (Prairies); 41, 47, 53 (Ontario); 59, 65, 71 (Quebec); 77, 83, 89 (Atlantic).

FIGURE 9.1

CALCULATION OF THE PROPORTION OF INCOME SPENT ON CHILDREN

Client name: _____

A Year	B Age of First Child	C[a] Cost of First Child (%)	D Age of Second Child	E[a] Cost of Second Child (%)	F Age of Third Child	G[a] Cost of Third Child (%)	H[b] Child Care (%)	I[c] Housing (%)	J[d] Total Cost (%)

[a] From child cost tables by income level: B.C. - Tables 1, 7, 13; Prairies - 19, 25, 31; Ontario - 37, 43, 49; Quebec - 55, 61, 67; Atlantic - 73, 79, 85.

[b] From child care cost tables by income level: B.C. - Tables 4, 10, 16; Prairies - 22, 28, 34; Ontario - 40, 46, 52; Quebec - 58, 64, 70; Atlantic - 76, 82, 88.

[c] From note b in total cost tables by income level: B.C. - Tables 5, 11, 17; Prairies - 23, 29, 35; Ontario - 41, 47, 53; Quebec - 59, 65, 71; Atlantic - 77, 83, 89.

[d] Sum of C, E, G, H and I. Used in Column D of Figure 9.2.

FIGURE 9.2

CALCULATION OF THE CHILD COSTS FOR MAINTENANCE AWARDS

Client name: _____

Income of absent parent in year of separation: $ _____ (A)

B Year	C Projected Income	D[a] Cost of Children (%)	E Annual Child Maintenance (CxD) / 100	(in base year dollars)
_____ [base] (A)	_____	_____	_____	
_____ (A x 1.02)	_____	_____	_____	
_____ (A x 1.04)	_____	_____	_____	
_____ (A x 1.06)	_____	_____	_____	
_____ (A x 1.08)	_____	_____	_____	
_____ (A x 1.10)	_____	_____	_____	
_____ (A x 1.13)	_____	_____	_____	
_____ (A x 1.15)	_____	_____	_____	
_____ (A x 1.17)	_____	_____	_____	
_____ (A x 1.20)	_____	_____	_____	
_____ (A x 1.22)	_____	_____	_____	
_____ (A x 1.24)	_____	_____	_____	
_____ (A x 1.27)	_____	_____	_____	
_____ (A x 1.29)	_____	_____	_____	
_____ (A x 1.32)	_____	_____	_____	
_____ (A x 1.35)	_____	_____	_____	
_____ (A x 1.37)	_____	_____	_____	
_____ (A x 1.40)	_____	_____	_____	
_____ (A x 1.43)	_____	_____	_____	

[a] From Figure 9.1.

FIGURE 9.3

CALCULATION OF THE PROPORTION OF INCOME SPENT ON JERILYN JOHNSON

Client name: _____ Claire Johnson

A Year	B Age of First Child	C Cost of First Child (%)	D Age of Second Child	E Cost of Second Child (%)	F Age of Third Child	G Cost of Third Child (%)	H Child Care (%)	I Housing (%)	J Total Cost (%)
1988	2	7					4	1	9[a]
1989	3	6					4	1	11
1990	4	5					4	1	10
1991	5	5					4	1	10
1992	6	5					3	1	9
1993	7	6					3	1	10
1994	8	6					3	1	10
1995	9	6					2	1	9
1996	10	6					2	1	9
1997	11	6					2	1	9
1998	12	6						1	7
1999	13	7						1	8
2000	14	7						1	8
2001	15	7						1	8
2002	16	7						1	8
2003	17	7						1	8
2004	18	8						1	6[b]

[a] Costs for the period April 18 - December 31.
[b] Costs for the period January 1 - September 21 (Jerilyn's 18th birthday).

74

Figure 9.4

Calculation of Maintenance for Johnsons

Client name: **Claire Johnson**

Income of absent parent in year of separation: $ **26,000** (A)

B Year		C Projected Income	D[a] Cost of Children (%)	E Annual Child Maintenance (CxD) / 100
1988	(A)	26,000	9	2,340
1989	(A x 1.02)	26,520	11	2,917
1990	(A x 1.04)	27,040	10	2,704
1991	(A x 1.06)	27,560	10	2,756
1992	(A x 1.08)	28,080	9	2,527
1993	(A x 1.10)	28,600	10	2,860
1994	(A x 1.13)	29,380	10	2,938
1995	(A x 1.15)	29,990	9	2,699
1996	(A x 1.17)	30,420	9	2,738
1997	(A x 1.20)	31,200	9	2,808
1998	(A x 1.22)	31,720	7	2,220
1999	(A x 1.24)	32,240	8	2,579
2000	(A x 1.27)	33,020	8	2,642
2001	(A x 1.29)	33,540	8	2,683
2002	(A x 1.32)	34,320	8	2,746
2003	(A x 1.35)	35,100	8	2,808
2004	(A x 1.37)	35,620	6	2,137
	(A x 1.40)			
	(A x 1.43)			

[a] From Figure 9.3.

Figure 9.5

Calculation of the Proportion of Income Spent on the Olson Children

Client name: Bill Olson

A Year	B Age of First Child	C Cost of First Child (%)	D Age of Second Child	E Cost of Second Child (%)	F Age of Third Child	G Cost of Third Child (%)	H Child Care (%)	I Housing (%)	J[a] Total Cost (%)
1988	8	9	4	8					17
1989	9	9	5	9					18
1990	10	9	6	9					18
1991	11	10	7	9					19
1992	12	10	8	9					19
1993	13	11	9	10					21
1994	14	12	10	10					22
1995	15	13	11	10					23
1996	16	13	12	10					23
1997	17	14	13	10					24
1998	18	11[b]	14	10					21
1999			15	10					10
2000			16	11					11
2001			17	13					13
2002			18	2[c]					2

[a] Sum of C, E, H and I. Used in Column D of Figure 9.6.
[b] Child costs for period January 1 - October 6 (Kelly's 18th birthday)
[c] Child costs for period January 1 - February 17 (Kim's 18th birthday)

Figure 9.6

Calculation of Maintenance for Olson Children

Client name: __Bill Olson__

Income of absent parent in year of separation: $ __44,000__ (A)

B Year		C Projected Income	D[a] Cost of Children (%)	E Annual Child Maintenance (CxD) / 100
1988	(A)	44,000	17	3,067[b]
1989	(A x 1.02)	44,880	18	8,078
1990	(A x 1.04)	45,760	18	8,237
1991	(A x 1.06)	46,640	19	8,862
1992	(A x 1.08)	47,520	19	9,029
1993	(A x 1.10)	48,400	21	10,164
1994	(A x 1.13)	49,720	22	10,938
1995	(A x 1.15)	50,600	23	11,638
1996	(A x 1.17)	51,480	23	11,840
1997	(A x 1.20)	52,800	24	12,672
1998	(A x 1.22)	53,680	21	11,273
1999	(A x 1.24)	54,560	10	5,456
2000	(A x 1.27)	55,880	11	6,147
2001	(A x 1.29)	56,760	13	7,379
2002	(A x 1.32)	58,080	2	1,162
	(A x 1.35)			
	(A x 1.37)			
	(A x 1.40)			
	(A x 1.43)			

[a] From Figure 9.5
[b] Child maintenance for the period August 3 (date of separation) - December 31.

CHAPTER 10

THE PRESENT VALUE OF CHILD REARING COSTS

In this chapter we present work sheets and instructions for using the information in Chapters 3 to 7 to determine the present value of child costs incurred in future periods. Persons who might find this information useful include couples who wish to set aside money to cover all or part of future child rearing costs. These work sheets can assist families to establish savings goals. For example, if one or both parents choose to reduce their labour force activities to be able to spend more time with the children, they may want to set aside sufficient funds to meet child rearing costs incurred during those years, usually while children are of pre-school age, when income is temporarily low. Family law specialists and divorce mediators may also find this information useful in those instances where they need to establish the current value of future child rearing costs in marital property settlements where child support is awarded as a lump sum.

PRESENT VALUE CALCULATIONS

Saving implies deferring the purchase of goods and services today in order to buy goods and services in a future period. However, a dollar spent in the future does not have the same value as a dollar spent today, for two reasons: 1) changes in prices (inflation), and 2) money's opportunity cost. Price increases devalue future money by decreasing the amount that a dollar can buy. For example, if a new bike costs $100 today, in ten years that same new bike, due to inflation, will cost more than $100. Thus, inflation, or increasing prices, results in a dollar today being worth more in purchasing power than a future dollar.

The second reason that a future dollar and a dollar today are not of commensurate value is that money has an opportunity cost. Opportunity cost refers to the value of a resource in its "second-best" use. Interest rates are often used to reflect money's opportunity cost. One can spend money today, but in doing so, one "loses" the interest that would have been received had the money been saved (the second best alternative to spending). The higher the interest rate, the more "future dollars" one gives up by spending it today. Or alternatively stated, the higher the interest rate, the fewer "today dollars" one needs to invest in order to meet future consumption needs.

Since "future dollars" and "today dollars" are not equivalent in value, adjustments must be made when planning for future spending to translate all the dollars involved into today's dollars. This adjustment is made taking into account both inflation and the opportunity cost of money. The process by which future dollars are translated into today's dollars is called discounting. Discounting is thus the tool used to determine *present values* such as calculating how many dollars must be invested today in order to be able to buy a certain market basket of goods and services in the future.

Consider, for example, a couple wanting to set aside enough money today to cover the first year cost of a child they plan on having in two years' time. Based on their expected income stream, they determine that during the first year the child will require a market basket of goods and services that would cost $3,000 if purchased today. However, the couple need not invest $3,000 today in order to meet these future child rearing costs. The principal investment needed to purchase that same market basket in two years is an amount sufficient to meet expected price increases less two years, interest. This amount is called the present value. So for example, if over the two-year period the expected interest rate is 10% and the inflation rate is 5% then the couple would need to deposit $2,721 today to cover costs in the first year of the child's life, i.e., $2,721 is the present value of $3,000 in two years at a 5% discount rate.[1]

COMPUTING PRESENT VALUES

Figure 10.1 is a work sheet which allows calculation of the present value of child costs. Before present values can be calculated, annual child costs as a percentage of income must be calculated by completing the work sheet in Figure 9.1..

Completing Figure 10.1 (page 83)

Step 1: Family Income in the Current Year - Item A

Total gross family income in the current year (not the year the child is expected to be born) is entered in Item A.

Step 2: Year - Column B

The first year entered is the current year (even if costs are being computed for a future child). The last year entered is the final year for which parents wish to compute child costs.

Step 3: Projected Income - Column C

Our estimates of child costs are based on the assumption that incomes increase over time. This increase in income partly explains our general finding that as a percentage of gross income, child costs are relatively constant over the life cycle. Had we assumed that family income remained constant over the life cycle, the cost of children as a percentage of income would increase more quickly. Thus, by building this growth trend in our simulations we assume that children share in real income growth.

Studies of long term income trends reveal that, on average, incomes annually increase by about 2%. Thus, we have included the figures to calculate a 2% annual increase in income in the work sheet.[2] To compute projected income, multiply A by the factor given for each year.

Step 4: Cost of Children - Column D

Child cost estimates are computed by completing the work sheet in Figure 9.1 and are then entered in Column D of Figure 10.1.

Step 5: Annual Cost of Children - Column E

Multiplying the percentage of income spent on children (Column D) by projected family income (Column C) yields the dollar cost of children in each year.

Step 6: Present Value Calculations - Column F

Present values are computed to translate all the dollar values into today's dollars. The numbers shown in Column F are those factors needed to calculate the present value of each year of child costs using a 3% discount rate. To calculate present value, multiply Column E by the factors given in Column F. Should a different discount rate be desired, the factors to calculate present values at discount rates of 1-5% are given in Appendix C Table C2.

Step 7: Total Present Value - Item G

The sum of all the present values in Column F yields a total which represents the number of dollars that need to be invested today to cover the child costs for the period in question.

CASE STUDY EXAMPLE

Case I: The Cost of a Future Child in the Atlantic Region

Case Specifics

Jack and Louise Adams were recently married in Halifax. They plan to start a family in three years. Jack is a computer technician and his current annual salary is $28,000. Louise has her own public relations firm and this year her salary was $35,000. A few months ago, Louise received an inheritance from a great-aunt. The couple has decided to set aside an amount from the inheritance that will cover the cost of their first child until s/he reaches age 18. They plan to purchase a house within the next year or two. Both Jack and Louise plan to continue working after the birth of their child, so full time child care expenses need to be included.

The work sheet shown in Figure 9.1 can be used in this case to calculate the total cost of the child. The completed work sheet for the Adams' child is shown in Figure 10.2. Figure 10.3 projects the Adams' income, calculates the present value of the annual amounts spent on the child, and shows the total of the present value calculations which is the amount that they need to set aside for their child.

Completing Figure 10.2 for the Adams (page 84)

Step 1: Year - Column A

Assuming the current year is 1988, the Adams are planning for a child to be born in 1991 (three years' time). Thus, 1991 is the first year entered. The year the child will turn 18, 2008, is the last year included.

Step 2: The Age of the First Child - Column B

The Adams want to cover expenses from birth to age 18, so these are the ages entered in Column B.

Step 3: The Cost of the First Child - Column C

The Adams' annual income totals $63,000, which places them in the upper-middle income category. Table 73 contains information on the proportion of income spent on children by upper-middle income families in the Atlantic provinces. The figures for the first child are entered in Column C. As only one child is involved, Columns D-G are left blank.

Step 4: Child Care - Column H

The Adams' child will require full time care. Figures for upper-middle Atlantic families' spending on child care are found in Table 76. The figures for one-child families with both parents employed are included in Column H.

Step 5: Housing - Column I

Jack and Louise plan to purchase a house before the child is born. As Table 77 indicates, upper-middle income Atlantic families who own their homes spend 2% of their income on each additional room. This number is included in Column I for each year. (See the housing sections of Chapters 3 to 7 for further discussion of the influence of children on housing expenditures.)

Step 6: Total Cost - Column J

The total percentage of income spent on children in each year is the sum of Columns C, H and I. These figures are entered in Column D of Figure 10.3.

Completing Figure 10.3 for the Adams (page 85)

Step 1: Family Income in the Current Year - Item A

This figure is total gross family income in the current year.

Step 2: Year - Column B

The first year is the current year, assumed to be 1988. The last year is the year that the Adams expect their child to reach age 18, 2008.

Step 3: Projected Income - Column C

Total family income is projected to grow at 2% per year.

Step 4: Cost of Children - Column D

These numbers are those taken from Column J in Figure 10.2. Note that no child costs are entered for the first three years. The costs begin in 1991, which is the year that the Adams expect their child to be born.

Step 5: Annual Cost of the Child - Column E

The percentage of income spent on the child is multiplied by the Adams' projected income in each year to get an annual dollar cost of the child.

Step 6: Calculating the Present Value - Column F

The present value is calculated by multiplying the child costs (Column E) by the discount factor (Column F). The discount factors in Column F assume a 3% discount rate. Should a different discount factor be desired, Appendix C Table C2 contains rates for 1-5%.

Step 7: Total Present Value - Item G

The sum of Column F yields total present value of the cost of raising the Adams child. This figure, $151,772, is the amount that Jake and Louise need to set aside from the inheritance to cover the cost of their first child to age 18.

END NOTES

1. The discount rate is the difference between the interest rate and the expected rate of inflation.
2. Two per cent was chosen as average. Other rates of income growth based on knowledge of families long term financial circumstances can be substituted here as appropriate.

Figure 10.1

Calculation of Present Value of Child Costs

Client name:_____

Family Income in the current year: $ _____ (A)

B	C	D[a]	E	F[b]
Year	Projected Income	Cost of Children (%	Annual Cost (CxD) / 100	Present Value
_____	(A) _____	_____	_____	(E) _____
_____	(A x 1.02) _____	_____	_____	(.971 x E) _____
_____	(A x 1.04) _____	_____	_____	(.943 x E) _____
_____	(A x 1.06) _____	_____	_____	(.915 x E) _____
_____	(A x 1.08) _____	_____	_____	(.888 x E) _____
_____	(A x 1.10) _____	_____	_____	(.863 x E) _____
_____	(A x 1.13) _____	_____	_____	(.837 x E) _____
_____	(A x 1.15) _____	_____	_____	(.813 x E) _____
_____	(A x 1.17) _____	_____	_____	(.789 x E) _____
_____	(A x 1.20) _____	_____	_____	(.766 x E) _____
_____	(A x 1.22) _____	_____	_____	(.744 x E) _____
_____	(A x 1.24) _____	_____	_____	(.722 x E) _____
_____	(A x 1.27) _____	_____	_____	(.701 x E) _____
_____	(A x 1.29) _____	_____	_____	(.681 x E) _____
_____	(A x 1.32) _____	_____	_____	(.661 x E) _____
_____	(A x 1.35) _____	_____	_____	(.642 x E) _____
_____	(A x 1.37) _____	_____	_____	(.623 x E) _____
_____	(A x 1.40) _____	_____	_____	(.605 x E) _____
_____	(A x 1.43) _____	_____	_____	(.587 x E) _____

G - TOTAL PRESENT VALUE: $ _____

[a] From work sheet that calculates total cost, *e.g.,* Figure 10.2.
[b] Discount rate of 3%

FIGURE 10.2

CALCULATION OF THE COST OF THE ADAMS CHILD

Client name: ____Jack and Louise Adams____

A Year	B Age of First Child	C Cost of First Child (%)	D Age of Second Child	E Cost of Second Child (%)	F Age of Third Child	G Cost of Third Child (%)	H Child Care (%)	I Housing (%)	J[a] Total Cost (%)
1991	1	8					3	2	13
1992	2	11					3	2	16
1993	3	10					3	2	15
1994	4	10					3	2	15
1995	5	10					2	2	14
1996	6	10					2	2	14
1997	7	10					2	2	14
1998	8	10					2	2	14
1999	9	10					2	2	14
2000	10	10					2	2	14
2001	11	11					2	2	15
2002	12	11						2	13
2003	13	12						2	14
2004	14	13						2	15
2005	15	14						2	16
2006	16	15						2	17
2007	17	16						2	18
2008	18	17						2	19

[a] Sum of C, H and I. Used in Column D of Figure 10.3.

Figure 10.3

Calculation of Present Value of Cost of Adams Child

Client name: __Louise and Jack Adams__

Family Income in the current year: $ __63,000__ (A)

B Year	C Projected Income	D Cost of Children (%)	E Annual Cost (CxD) / 100		F Present Value
1988	(A) 63,000			(E)	
1989	(A x 1.02) 64,260			(.971 x E)	
1990	(A x 1.04) 65,520			(.943 x E)	
1991	(A x 1.06) 66,780	13	8,681	(.915 x E)	7,943
1992	(A x 1.08) 68,040	16	10,886	(.888 x E)	9,667
1993	(A x 1.10) 69,300	15	10,395	(.863 x E)	8,971
1994	(A x 1.13) 71,190	15	10,679	(.837 x E)	8,938
1995	(A x 1.15) 72,450	14	10,143	(.813 x E)	8,246
1996	(A x 1.17) 73,710	14	10,319	(.789 x E)	8,142
1997	(A x 1.20) 75,600	14	10,584	(.766 x E)	8,107
1998	(A x 1.22) 76,860	14	10,760	(.744 x E)	8,005
1999	(A x 1.24) 78,120	14	10,937	(.722 x E)	7,897
2000	(A x 1.27) 80,010	14	11,201	(.701 x E)	7,852
2001	(A x 1.29) 81,270	15	12,191	(.681 x E)	8,302
2002	(A x 1.32) 83,160	13	10,811	(.661 x E)	7,146
2003	(A x 1.35) 85,050	14	11,907	(.642 x E)	7,644
2004	(A x 1.37) 86,310	15	12,947	(.623 x E)	8,066
2005	(A x 1.40) 88,200	16	14,112	(.605 x E)	8,538
2006	(A x 1.43) 90,090	17	15,315	(.587 x E)	8,990
2007	(A x 1.46) 91,980	18	16,556	(.570 x E)	9,437
2008	(A x 1.49) 93,870	19	17,835	(.554 x E)	9,881

G - TOTAL PRESENT VALUE: $ 151,772

Part II

Child Costs by Family Income Level by Region

Table 1

Percentage of Gross Income Spent on Each Child by Upper-Middle Income[a] British Columbia Families, EXCLUDING Housing and Child Care Expenditures[b]

Age of Youngest Child	Percentage of Gross Income		
	First Child	Second Child	Third Child
1	16%	18%	11%
2	12	12	8
3	9	10	6
4	8	10	8
5	8	11	10
6	9	11	11
7	9	12	13
8	10	13	13
9	10	13	14
10	11	13	14
11	12	13	14
12	12	13	13
13	13	12	13
14	13	12	12
15	13	12	12[c]
16	14	12	12[c]
17	14	13[c]	12[d]
18	14	13[c]	12[d]
Average cost	12%	12%	12%

[a] Upper-middle income families include those families with gross incomes of $45,000 to $100,000 per year in 1988

[b] Excludes increased spending on durable goods, such as vehicles, appliances, and furniture, due to the presence of children.

[c] First child left home.

[d] Second child left home.

TABLE 2

PERCENTAGE OF ANNUAL CHILD REARING COSTS, EXCLUDING HOUSING AND CHILD CARE, BY CATEGORY OF SPENDING: UPPER-MIDDLE INCOME BRITISH COLUMBIA FAMILIES

Age of Youngest Child	Spending Category							
	Food at Home	Clothing	Utilities	Household Operation	Trans-portation	Health Care	Education Related	Miscl.
First Child								
1	49%	3%	16%	0%	17%	7%	0%	8%
2	43	4	13	6	23	4	0	7
3	49	7	12	9	22	1	0	0
4	54	10	11	7	16	1	0	1
5	56	11	11	6	12	1	1	2
6	56	11	10	5	8	2	3	5
7	55	11	9	4	6	3	4	8
8	54	10	8	4	5	4	5	10
9	53	9	8	4	4	4	6	12
10	52	9	7	4	4	4	7	13
11	50	11	6	4	4	4	7	14
12	48	15	5	5	5	4	8	10
13	46	17	5	5	6	4	8	9
14	45	19	4	5	7	4	9	7
15	44	21	4	6	8	4	9	4
16	43	22	3	7	9	3	9	4
17	42	25	3	7	10	3	10	0
18	41	25	2	8	11	2	10	1
Average cost	49%	13%	8%	5%	10%	3%	5%	6%
Second Child[a]								
1	43%	5%	17%	0%	20%	6%	0%	9%
2	42	6	16	1	22	4	0	9
3	47	15	15	3	19	0	0	1
4	50	20	14	3	13	0	0	0
5	53	22	13	3	8	1	0	0
6	55	23	12	2	5	3	0	0
7	55	22	10	1	2	4	0	6
8	55	20	9	1	1	4	0	10
9	56	18	9	1	0	5	0	11
10	57	16	8	1	0	6	0	12
11	58	14	7	1	0	6	0	14
12	60	13	7	2	1	6	0	11
13	61	13	6	2	1	6	0	11
14	60	17	5	3	2	5	0	8
15	59	20	4	4	3	5	0	5
16	57	24	3	5	5	4	0	2
17	44	24	3	7	10	3	9	0
18	43	24	2	8	11	2	10	0
Average cost	53%	18%	9%	3%	7%	4%	1%	6%

TABLE 2 (continued)

**PERCENTAGE OF ANNUAL CHILD REARING COSTS, EXCLUDING HOUSING AND
CHILD CARE, BY CATEGORY OF SPENDING:
UPPER-MIDDLE INCOME BRITISH COLUMBIA FAMILIES**

Age of Youngest Child	Food at Home	Clothing	Utilities	Household Operation	Trans- portation	Health Care	Education Related	Miscl.
Third Child[a]								
1	33%	13%	19%	0%	15%	7%	0%	13%
2	38	15	21	0	13	4	0	9
3	36	46	18	0	1	0	0	0
4	37	51	12	0	0	0	0	10
5	41	50	10	0	0	0	0	0
6	44	47	8	0	0	0	0	1
7	47	43	8	0	0	2	0	0
8	49	37	7	0	0	3	0	4
9	51	31	6	0	0	5	0	7
10	53	26	6	0	0	5	0	10
11	56	22	6	0	0	6	0	10
12	59	19	5	0	0	6	0	11
13	63	16	5	0	0	6	1	9
14	66	13	4	0	0	6	3	8
15	61	19	4	3	3	5	0	5
16	60	23	3	4	4	4	0	5
17	48	23	2	7	9	3	9	8
18	48	23	2	7	10	2	9	1
Average cost	49%	29%	8%	1%	3%	4%	1%	6%

[a] Assumes children are spaced two years apart.

Table 3

AVERAGE PERCENTAGE OF GROSS INCOME SPENT BY UPPER-MIDDLE INCOME[a]
BRITISH COLUMBIA FAMILIES FOR HOUSING OVER THE LIFE CYCLE

Housing Category	One-Child Family	Two-Child Family	Three-Child Family
Homeowners	14%	12%	11%
Renters	15%	15%	14%

[a] Upper-middle income families include those families with gross incomes of $45,000 to $100,000 per year in 1988.

TABLE 4

PERCENTAGE OF GROSS INCOME SPENT BY UPPER-MIDDLE INCOME
BRITISH COLUMBIA FAMILIES FOR CHILD CARE EXPENDITURES
BY PARENTAL EMPLOYMENT STATUS

Age of Youngest Child	One Child		Two Children		Three Children	
	Both Parents Employed	One Parent Employed	Both Parents Employed	One Parent Employed	Both Parents Employed	One Parent Employed
1	4%	*	3%	*	2%	*
2	3	*	3	*	2	*
3	3	*	2	*	2	*
4	3	*	2	*	2	*
5	3	*	2	*	2	*
6	3	*	2	*	2	*
7	2	*	2	*	2	*
8	2	*	2	*	1	*
9	2	*	2	*	1	*
10	2	*	2	*	1	*
11	2	*	2	*	1	*
Average Cost	3%	*	2%	*	2%	*

* Less than 1% of gross income annually.

TABLE 5

PERCENTAGE OF GROSS INCOME SPENT BY UPPER-MIDDLE INCOME[a] BRITISH COLUMBIA FAMILIES ON CHILD REARING COSTS INCLUDING HOUSING[b] AND CHILD CARE – HOME OWNERS & BOTH PARENTS EMPLOYED[c]

Age of Youngest Child	Percentage of Gross Income		
	One-Child Family	Two-Child Family	Three-Child Family
1	21%	32%	34%
2	16	25	32
3	13	22	31
4	12	23	34
5	12	24	37
6	13	25	40
7	12	26	43
8	13	28	42
9	13	29	44
10	14	29	44
11	15	30	43
12	13	28	42
13	14	27	42
14	14	28	41
15	14	28	27[d]
16	15	28	27[d]
17	15	14[e]	13[e]
18	15	14[e]	13[e]
Average cost	14%	25%[f]	33%[f]

[a] Upper-middle income families include those families with incomes of $45,000 to $100,000 per year in 1988.

[b] 1% of gross income is added to cover the cost of an additional room for home owners, add 1% gross income for the cost of an additional room for renters.

[c] Excludes increased spending on durable goods, such as vehicles, appliances, and furniture, due to the presence of children.

[d] First child left home.

[e] Second child left home.

[f] Averages include years prior to last child's birth when other children were present.

TABLE 6

PERCENTAGE OF GROSS INCOME SAVED BY UPPER-MIDDLE INCOME BRITISH COLUMBIA FAMILIES OF DIFFERENT COMPOSITION OVER THE LIFE CYCLE

Age of Adult Male	Childless Couple	Age of First Child	One-Child Family	Age of Second Child	Two-Child Family	Age of Third Child	Three-Child Family
28	31%						
29	32	1	24%				
30	32	2	30				
31	32	3	31	1	25%		
32	33	4	31	2	31		
33	33	5	31	3	32	1	26%
34	33	6	31	4	31	2	31
35	33	7	31	5	31	3	32
36	33	8	31	6	30	4	31
37	34	9	31	7	30	5	30
38	34	10	30	8	29	6	29
39	34	11	30	9	29	7	28
40	34	12	30	10	28	8	28
41	34	13	30	11	28	9	27
42	35	14	31	12	28	10	27
43	35	15	31	13	28	11	27
44	35	16	31	14	28	12	27
45	36	17	31	15	28	13	27
46	36	18	32	16	29	14	27
47	36			17	31	15	29
48	37			18	32	16	29
49	37					17	33
50	38					18	33
Average	34%		30%		29%[a]		29%[a]

[a] Averages include years prior to last child's birth when other children were present.

TABLE 7

PERCENTAGE OF GROSS INCOME SPENT ON EACH CHILD
BY MIDDLE INCOME[a] BRITISH COLUMBIA FAMILIES,
EXCLUDING HOUSING AND CHILD CARE EXPENDITURES[b]

Age of Youngest Child	Percentage of Gross Income		
	First Child	Second Child	Third Child
1	10%	12%	9%
2	10	10	6
3	8	8	5
4	7	9	7
5	7	9	9
6	7	9	10
7	7	10	11
8	8	11	11
9	8	11	11
10	8	11	12
11	9	11	11
12	9	0	11
13	10	0	10
14	10	9	10
15	10	9	9[c]
16	10	9	9[c]
17	10	10[c]	9[d]
18	11	10[c]	10[d]
Average cost	9%	11%	9%

[a] Middle income families include those families with gross incomes of $30,000 to $45,000 per year in 1988.
[b] Excludes increased spending on durable goods, such as vehicles, appliances, and furniture, due to the presence of children.
[c] First child left home.
[d] Second child left home.

TABLE 8

PERCENTAGE OF ANNUAL CHILD REARING COSTS, EXCLUDING HOUSING AND CHILD CARE, BY CATEGORY OF SPENDING: MIDDLE INCOME BRITISH COLUMBIA FAMILIES

Age of Youngest Child	Spending Category							
	Food at Home	Clothing	Utilities	Household Operation	Trans-portation	Health Care	Education Related	Miscl.
First Child								
1	40%	4%	12%	0%	19%	9%	0%	16%
2	47	4	13	5	22	4	0	5
3	53	8	12	7	20	0	0	0
4	58	11	11	5	14	0	0	1
5	62	13	10	4	9	1	1	0
6	62	13	9	3	5	2	2	4
7	62	13	9	2	3	3	3	5
8	61	12	8	2	1	4	4	8
9	60	11	7	2	1	4	5	10
10	60	10	6	2	1	5	6	10
11	59	11	6	2	1	5	7	9
12	56	14	5	3	2	5	7	8
13	54	17	4	3	3	4	8	7
14	53	19	3	4	4	4	8	5
15	52	20	3	5	5	4	9	2
16	51	22	2	5	6	3	10	1
17	49	23	2	6	8	2	10	0
18	47	24	1	7	9	2	10	0
Average cost	55%	14%	7%	4%	7%	3%	5%	5%
Second Child[a]								
1	35%	6%	21%	0%	22%	8%	0%	8%
2	46	7	16	0	21	4	0	6
3	50	16	15	2	17	0	0	0
4	52	22	13	2	11	0	0	0
5	56	24	12	1	6	1	0	0
6	59	25	11	0	2	2	0	0
7	59	24	10	0	0	4	0	3
8	59	22	9	0	0	4	0	6
9	59	20	8	0	0	5	0	8
10	60	18	7	0	0	6	0	9
11	62	16	7	0	0	6	0	9
12	65	14	6	0	0	6	0	9
13	68	13	5	0	0	6	0	8
14	68	16	4	1	0	6	0	5
15	67	19	3	2	0	5	0	4
16	66	22	2	3	2	4	0	1
17	51	22	1	6	8	2	9	1
18	49	24	1	7	9	2	10	0
Average cost	57%	18%	8%	1%	5%	4%	1%	4%

98

Table 8 (continued)

Percentage of Annual Child Rearing Costs, Excluding Housing and Child Care, by Category of Spending: Middle Income British Columbia Families

Age of Youngest Child	Food at Home	Clothing	Utilities	Household Operation	Trans- portation	Health Care	Education Related	Miscl.
Third Child[a]								
1	34%	13%	20%	0%	16%	8%	0%	9%
2	40	16	22	0	11	4	0	7
3	35	48	17	0	0	0	0	0
4	36	53	11	0	0	0	0	0
5	39	52	9	0	0	0	0	0
6	43	50	7	0	0	0	0	0
7	47	45	6	0	0	2	0	0
8	49	40	6	0	0	3	0	2
9	51	34	5	0	0	4	0	4
10	54	29	5	0	0	5	0	7
11	58	24	4	0	0	6	0	8
12	61	20	4	0	0	6	0	9
13	65	17	4	0	0	6	0	8
14	69	14	3	0	0	6	2	6
15	69	18	3	1	0	5	0	4
16	69	21	2	2	1	4	0	1
17	54	21	1	5	7	2	9	1
18	52	22	1	6	8	2	9	0
Average cost	51%	30%	7%	1%	2%	4%	1%	4%

[a] Assumes children are spaced two years apart.

TABLE 9

AVERAGE PERCENTAGE OF GROSS INCOME SPENT BY MIDDLE INCOME[a] BRITISH COLUMBIA FAMILIES FOR HOUSING OVER THE LIFE CYCLE

Housing Category	One-Child Family	Two-Child Family	Three-Child Family
Home owners	12%	10%	8%
Renters	16%	15%	14%

[a] Middle income families include those families with gross incomes of $30, 000 to $45,000 per year in 1988.

TABLE 10

PERCENTAGE OF GROSS INCOME SPENT BY MIDDLE INCOME BRITISH COLUMBIA FAMILIES FOR CHILD CARE EXPENDITURES BY PARENTAL EMPLOYMENT STATUS

Age of Youngest Child	One Child Both Parents Employed	One Child One Parent Employed	Two Children Both Parents Employed	Two Children One Parent Employed	Three Children Both Parents Employed	Three Children One Parent Employed
1	4%	1%	4%	1%	3%	1%
2	4	*	3	*	2	*
3	3	*	2	*	2	*
4	3	*	2	*	2	*
5	3	*	2	*	2	*
6	3	*	2	*	2	*
7	3	*	2	*	1	*
8	3	*	2	*	1	*
9	3	*	2	*	1	*
10	3	*	1	*	1	*
11	2	*	1	*	1	*
Average cost	3%	*	2%	*	2%	*

* Less than 1% of gross income annually.

Table 11

Percentage of Gross Income Spent by Middle Income[a] British Columbia Families on Child Rearing Costs INCLUDING Housing[b] and Child Care –
HOME OWNERS & BOTH PARENTS EMPLOYED[c]

Age of Youngest Child	Percentage of Gross Income		
	One-Child Family	Two-Child Family	Three-Child Family
1	15%	26%	30%
2	15	22	27
3	12	19	26
4	11	20	29
5	11	20	32
6	11	21	34
7	11	22	35
8	12	23	35
9	12	24	36
10	12	23	36
11	12	24	35
12	10	22	33
13	11	22	32
14	11	21	33
15	11	21	21[d]
16	11	22	21[d]
17	11	11[d]	10[e]
18	12	11[d]	11[e]
Average cost	12%	20%[f]	27%[f]

[a] Middle income families include those families with incomes of $30,000 to $45,000 per year in 1988.

[b] 1% of gross income has been added to cover the cost of an additional room for home owners, add 1% gross income for the cost of an additional room for renters.

[c] Excludes increased spending on durable goods, such as vehicles, appliances, and furniture, due to the presence of children.

[d] First child left home.

[e] Second child left home.

[f] Averages include years prior to last child's birth when other children were present.

TABLE 12

PERCENTAGE OF GROSS INCOME SAVED BY MIDDLE INCOME BRITISH COLUMBIA FAMILIES OF DIFFERENT COMPOSITION OVER THE LIFE CYCLE

Age of Adult Male	Childless Couple	Age of First Child	One-Child Family	Age of Second Child	Two-Child Family	Age of Third Child	Three-Child Family
28	23%						
29	23	1	17%				
30	24	2	22				
31	24	3	23	1	18%		
32	24	4	23	2	23		
33	24	5	23	3	23	1	19%
34	24	6	23	4	23	2	23
35	25	7	23	5	22	3	23
36	25	8	22	6	22	4	23
37	25	9	22	7	22	5	22
38	25	10	22	8	21	6	21
39	25	11	22	9	21	7	21
40	25	12	22	10	21	8	20
41	26	13	22	11	21	9	20
42	26	14	22	12	20	10	20
43	26	15	22	13	21	11	19
44	26	16	23	14	21	12	19
45	27	17	23	15	21	13	19
46	27	18	23	16	21	14	19
47	27			17	24	15	21
48	28			18	24	16	22
49	28					17	24
50	28					18	25
Average	26%		23%		22%[a]		21%[a]

[a] Averages include years prior to last child's birth when other children were present.

TABLE 13

PERCENTAGE OF GROSS INCOME SPENT ON EACH CHILD BY LOWER-MIDDLE
INCOME[a] BRITISH COLUMBIA FAMILIES ON CHILD REARING COSTS
EXCLUDING HOUSING AND CHILD CARE EXPENDITURES[b]

Age of Youngest Child	Percentage of Gross Income		
	First Child	Second Child	Third Child
1	9%	10%	6%
2	7	8	5
3	6	7	4
4	5	7	6
5	5	7	7
6	5	8	8
7	6	8	8
8	6	8	9
9	6	9	9
10	6	8	9
11	6	8	9
12	6	8	8
13	7	7	8
14	7	7	7
15	7	7	7[c]
16	7	7	6[c]
17	7	7[c]	7[d]
18	8	7[c]	7[d]
Average cost	6%	8%	7%

[a] Lower-middle income families include those families with gross incomes of $15,000 to $30,000 per year in 1988.
[b] Excludes increased spending on durable goods, such as vehicles, appliances, and furniture, due to the presence of children.
[c] First child left home.
[d] Second child left home.

TABLE 14

Percentage of Annual Child Rearing Costs, Excluding Housing and Child Care, by Category of Spending: Lower-Middle Income British Columbia Families

Age of Youngest Child	Food at Home	Clothing	Utilities	Household Operation	Trans-portation	Health Care	Education Related	Miscl.
First Child								
1	56%	6%	17%	0%	12%	7%	0%	2%
2	53	5	13	3	20	4	0	2
3	58	9	12	4	17	0	0	0
4	64	13	10	3	10	0	0	0
5	69	15	10	1	5	0	0	0
6	72	16	9	0	1	1	1	0
7	70	15	7	0	0	2	2	4
8	69	14	6	0	0	3	3	5
9	68	13	5	0	0	4	4	6
10	67	12	5	0	0	4	5	7
11	68	11	4	0	0	5	6	6
12	67	13	3	0	0	5	7	5
13	66	16	3	1	0	4	7	3
14	65	18	2	1	0	4	8	2
15	63	19	1	2	1	3	9	2
16	61	21	0	3	2	3	9	1
17	58	22	0	4	4	2	10	0
18	56	22	0	5	6	1	10	0
Average cost	64%	14%	6%	2%	4%	3%	5%	3%
Second Child[a]								
1	50%	6%	18%	0%	14%	7%	0%	5%
2	49	8	16	0	19	4	0	4
3	53	18	15	0	15	0	0	0
4	55	24	13	0	8	0	0	0
5	59	27	12	0	2	0	0	0
6	61	28	10	0	0	2	0	0
7	62	26	9	0	0	3	0	0
8	61	24	8	0	0	4	0	3
9	62	22	7	0	0	5	0	4
10	63	20	6	0	0	5	0	6
11	66	18	5	0	0	6	0	5
12	69	16	4	0	0	6	0	5
13	72	14	3	0	0	6	0	5
14	74	14	2	0	0	5	0	5
15	75	17	1	0	0	5	0	2
16	76	20	0	0	0	3	0	1
17	60	21	0	4	4	2	9	0
18	57	22	0	5	6	1	10	0
Average cost	62%	19%	7%	1%	4%	4%	1%	3%

TABLE 14 (continued)

PERCENTAGE OF ANNUAL CHILD REARING COSTS, EXCLUDING HOUSING AND CHILD CARE, BY CATEGORY OF SPENDING: LOWER-MIDDLE INCOME BRITISH COLUMBIA FAMILIES

Age of Youngest Child	Spending Category							
	Food at Home	Clothing	Utilities	Household Operation	Trans- portation	Health Care	Education Related	Miscl.
Third Child[a]								
1	39%	14%	23%	0%	9%	9%	0%	6%
2	42	18	23	0	8	4	0	5
3	33	51	16	0	0	0	0	0
4	34	56	10	0	0	0	0	0
5	37	55	7	0	0	0	0	1
6	41	53	6	0	0	0	0	0
7	45	49	5	0	0	1	0	0
8	49	44	4	0	0	2	0	1
9	52	38	3	0	0	4	0	3
10	55	32	3	0	0	5	0	5
11	59	27	3	0	0	5	0	6
12	63	23	2	0	0	6	0	6
13	68	19	2	0	0	6	0	5
14	73	16	1	0	0	5	1	4
15	77	15	1	0	0	5	0	2
16	78	19	0	0	0	3	0	0
17	62	20	0	4	3	2	9	0
18	60	21	0	4	5	1	9	0
Average cost	54%	32%	6%	0%	1%	3%	1%	2%

[a] Assumes children are spaced two years apart.

TABLE 15

AVERAGE PERCENTAGE OF GROSS INCOME SPENT BY LOWER-MIDDLE INCOME[a] BRITISH COLUMBIA FAMILIES FOR HOUSING OVER THE LIFE CYCLE

Housing Category	One-Child Family	Two-Child Family	Three-Child Family
Home owners	9%	7%	6%
Renters	16%	16%	15%

[a] Lower-middle income families include those families with gross incomes of $15, 000 to $30,000 per year in 1988.

TABLE 16

PERCENTAGE OF GROSS INCOME SPENT BY LOWER-MIDDLE INCOME BRITISH COLUMBIA FAMILIES FOR CHILD CARE EXPENDITURES BY PARENTAL EMPLOYMENT STATUS

Age of Youngest Child	One Child Both Parents Employed	One Child One Parent Employed	Two Children Both Parents Employed	Two Children One Parent Employed	Three Children Both Parents Employed	Three Children One Parent Employed
1	4%	1%	3%	1%	3%	1%
2	4	*	3	*	2	*
3	3	*	2	*	2	*
4	3	*	2	*	2	*
5	3	*	2	*	1	*
6	3	*	2	*	1	*
7	3	*	2	*	1	*
8	3	*	2	*	1	*
9	2	*	2	*	1	*
10	2	*	2	*	1	*
11	2	*	2	*	1	*
Average cost	3%	*	2%	*	1%	*

* Less than 1% of gross income annually.

TABLE 17

PERCENTAGE OF GROSS INCOME SPENT BY LOWER-MIDDLE INCOME[a] BRITISH COLUMBIA FAMILIES ON CHILD REARING COSTS INCLUDING HOUSING[b] AND CHILD CARE – HOME OWNERS & BOTH PARENTS EMPLOYED[c]

Age of Youngest Child	Percentage of Gross Income		
	One-Child Family	Two-Child Family	Three-Child Family
1	14%	21%	24%
2	12	18	22
3	10	16	22
4	9	16	25
5	9	17	25
6	9	18	26
7	10	18	27
8	10	18	27
9	9	19	28
10	9	18	28
11	9	19	27
12	7	17	25
13	8	16	25
14	8	16	25
15	8	16	16[d]
16	8	17	15[d]
17	8	8[d]	8[e]
18	9	8[d]	8[e]
Average cost	9%	16%[f]	21%[f]

[a] Lower-middle income families include those families with incomes of $15,000 to $30,000 per year in 1988.
[b] 1% of gross income is added to cover the cost of an additional room for home owners, add 1% gross income for the cost of an additional room for renters.
[c] Excludes increased spending on durable goods, such as vehicles, appliances, and furniture, due to the presence of children.
[d] First child left home.
[e] Second child left home.
[f] Averages include years prior to last child's birth when other children were present.

TABLE 18

PERCENTAGE OF GROSS INCOME SAVED BY LOWER-MIDDLE INCOME
BRITISH COLUMBIA FAMILIES OF DIFFERENT COMPOSITION OVER THE LIFE CYCLE

Age of Adult Male	Childless Couple	Age of First Child	One - Child Family	Age of Second Child	Two - Child Family	Age of Third Child	Three - Child Family
28	16%						
29	16	1	12%				
30	16	2	15				
31	16	3	16	1	12%		
32	17	4	16	2	15		
33	17	5	16	3	16	1	13%
34	17	6	16	4	16	2	16
35	17	7	15	5	15	3	16
36	17	8	15	6	15	4	16
37	17	9	15	7	15	5	15
38	17	10	15	8	14	6	15
39	17	11	15	9	14	7	14
40	18	12	15	10	14	8	14
41	18	13	15	11	14	9	13
42	18	14	15	12	14	10	13
43	18	15	15	13	14	11	13
44	18	16	16	14	14	12	13
45	19	17	16	15	14	13	13
46	19	18	16	16	14	14	13
47	19			17	16	15	14
48	19			18	16	16	15
49	20					17	17
50	20					18	17
Average	18%		15%		28%[a]		14%[a]

[a] Averages include years prior to last child's birth when other children were present.

TABLE 19

PERCENTAGE OF GROSS INCOME SPENT ON EACH CHILD BY UPPER-MIDDLE INCOME[a] PRAIRIE FAMILIES, EXCLUDING HOUSING AND CHILD CARE EXPENDITURES[b]

Age of Youngest Child	Percentage of Gross Income		
	First Child	Second Child	Third Child
1	7%	7%	9%
2	10	10	9
3	9	11	11
4	9	10	11
5	9	10	11
6	9	10	11
7	9	10	12
8	9	10	12
9	9	10	12
10	10	10	11
11	10	10	11
12	11	11	12
13	12	11	12
14	13	11	12
15	14	12	12[c]
16	15	14	13[c]
17	16	16[c]	13[d]
18	17	16[c]	14[d]
Average cost	11%	11%	12%

[a] Upper-middle income families include those families with gross incomes of $45,000 to $100,000 per year in 1988.

[b] Excludes increased spending on durable goods, such as vehicles, appliances, and furniture, due to the presence of children.

[c] First child left home.

[d] Second child left home.

TABLE 20

PERCENTAGE OF ANNUAL CHILD REARING COSTS, EXCLUDING HOUSING AND CHILD CARE, BY CATEGORY OF SPENDING: UPPER-MIDDLE INCOME PRAIRIE FAMILIES

Age of Youngest Child	Spending Category							
	Food at Home	Clothing	Utilities	Household Operation	Trans-portation	Health Care	Education Related	Miscl.
First Child								
1	55%	7%	17%	0%	5%	0%	5%	11%
2	47	6	14	0	13	0	5	15
3	51	8	15	0	11	0	5	20
4	54	10	14	0	11	0	6	5
5	57	11	13	0	9	0	7	3
6	58	12	12	0	8	1	7	2
7	59	12	11	0	7	2	8	1
8	58	11	10	2	7	3	9	0
9	57	11	9	3	7	3	9	1
10	55	10	9	5	8	3	10	0
11	54	9	8	6	9	3	11	0
12	50	12	8	6	10	3	11	0
13	47	15	7	6	11	3	11	0
14	43	17	7	6	12	3	11	1
15	40	19	7	6	12	2	11	3
16	37	20	7	6	13	2	11	4
17	35	21	6	6	14	2	10	6
18	33	23	6	6	15	1	10	6
Average cost								
	49%	13%	10%	3%	10%	2%	9%	4%
Second Child[a]								
1	57%	15%	18%	0%	0%	0%	0%	10%
2	45	12	13	0	0	0	0	30
3	47	17	13	0	0	0	0	23
4	53	21	12	0	0	0	0	14
5	59	26	10	0	0	0	0	5
6	62	27	9	0	0	0	0	2
7	64	26	7	0	0	2	1	0
8	64	25	6	0	0	3	2	0
9	64	23	6	0	0	3	4	0
10	64	20	5	0	0	4	6	1
11	63	18	5	2	0	4	8	0
12	65	15	5	3	0	4	10	0
13	62	12	5	4	0	4	11	2
14	60	11	5	5	3	3	13	0
15	54	15	5	5	5	3	14	0
16	49	18	5	5	7	2	14	0
17	36	21	7	6	14	2	10	4
18	34	22	7	5	15	1	10	6
Average cost								
	56%	19%	8%	2%	2%	2%	6%	5%

Table 20 (continued)

Percentage of Annual Child Rearing Costs, Excluding Housing and Child Care, by Category of Spending: Upper-Middle Income Prairie Families

Age of Youngest Child	Food at Home	Clothing	Utilities	Household Operation	Trans-portation	Health Care	Education Related	Miscl.
Third Child[a]								
1	31%	25%	4%	0%	0%	0%	0%	40%
2	28	24	6	0	0	0	0	42
3	32	33	7	0	0	0	0	28
4	38	40	5	0	0	0	0	17
5	44	45	4	0	0	0	0	7
6	49	46	3	0	0	0	0	2
7	53	44	2	0	0	0	0	1
8	56	40	2	0	0	2	0	0
9	59	36	2	0	0	3	0	0
10	63	31	2	0	0	4	0	0
11	65	26	2	0	0	4	2	1
12	65	21	3	1	0	4	5	1
13	65	17	3	3	0	4	8	0
14	65	13	3	4	0	4	11	0
15	56	14	5	4	5	3	13	0
16	51	17	5	4	6	2	14	1
17	40	19	7	5	13	1	10	5
18	39	21	7	4	14	1	10	4
Average cost								
	50%	28%	4%	1%	2%	2%	4%	8%

[a] Assumes children are spaced two years apart.

Table 21

Average Percentage of Gross Income Spent by Upper-Middle Income[a] British Columbia Families for Housing over the Life Cycle

Housing Category	One-Child Family	Two-Child Family	Three-Child Family
Home owners	16%	15%	14%
Renters	19%	18%	17%

[a] Upper-middle income families include those families with gross incomes of $45, 000 to $100,000 per year in 1988.

TABLE 22

PERCENTAGE OF GROSS INCOME SPENT BY UPPER-MIDDLE INCOME PRAIRIE FAMILIES FOR CHILD CARE EXPENDITURES BY PARENTAL EMPLOYMENT STATUS

Age of Youngest Child	One Child		Two Children		Three Children	
	Both Parents Employed	One Parent Employed	Both Parents Employed	One Parent Employed	Both Parents Employed	One Parent Employed
1	3%	1%	4%	1%	4%	1%
2	3	1	3	1	3	*
3	2	*	3	*	3	*
4	3	*	3	*	2	*
5	2	*	2	*	2	*
6	2	*	2	*	2	*
7	2	*	2	*	2	*
8	2	*	2	*	2	*
9	2	*	2	*	2	*
10	1	*	1	*	2	*
11	1	*	1	*	1	*
Average cost	2%	*	2%	*	2%	*

* Less than 1% of gross income annually.

TABLE 23

PERCENTAGE OF GROSS INCOME SPENT BY UPPER-MIDDLE INCOME[a] PRAIRIE FAMILIES ON CHILD REARING COSTS INCLUDING HOUSING[b] AND CHILD CARE – HOME OWNERS & BOTH PARENTS EMPLOYED[c]

Age of Youngest Child	Percentage of Gross Income		
	One-Child Family	Two-Child Family	Three-Child Family
1	11%	22%	36%
2	14	24	34
3	12	25	36
4	13	24	35
5	12	23	35
6	12	23	36
7	12	23	37
8	12	24	38
9	12	24	39
10	12	24	40
11	12	25	40
12	12	26	41
13	13	27	43
14	14	28	46
15	15	30	30 [d]
16	16	33	31 [d]
17	17	17 [d]	14 [e]
18	18	17 [d]	15 [e]
Average cost	13%	23% [f]	32%

[a] Upper-middle income families include those families with gross incomes of $45,000 to $100,000 per year in 1988.

[b] 1% of gross income is added to cover the cost of an additional room for home owners, add 1% gross income for the cost of an additional room for renters.

[c] Excludes increased spending on durable goods, such as vehicles, appliances, and furniture, due to the presence of children.

[d] First child left home.

[e] Second child left home.

[f] Averages include years prior to last child's birth when other children were present.

TABLE 24

PERCENTAGE OF GROSS INCOME SAVED BY UPPER-MIDDLE INCOME PRAIRIE FAMILIES OF DIFFERENT COMPOSITION OVER THE LIFE CYCLE

Age of Adult Male	Childless Couple	Age of First Child	One-Child Family	Age of Second Child	Two-Child Family	Age of Third Child	Three-Child Family
28	25%						
29	25	1	33%				
30	24	2	21				
31	24	3	20	1	30%		
32	24	4	21	2	19		
33	24	5	21	3	20	1	32%
34	24	6	22	4	21	2	22
35	24	7	23	5	23	3	23
36	25	8	24	6	25	4	25
37	25	9	24	7	26	5	27
38	26	10	24	8	26	6	29
39	26	11	25	9	26	7	29
40	27	12	25	10	26	8	30
41	28	13	25	11	26	9	30
42	28	14	25	12	25	10	28
43	29	15	25	13	25	11	27
44	30	16	25	14	24	12	26
45	31	17	24	15	23	13	24
46	32	18	24	16	22	14	22
47	33			17	26	15	24
48	34			18	26	16	23
49	35					17	28
50	36					18	28
Average	28%		24%		24%[a]		27%[a]

[a] Averages include years prior to last child's birth when other children were present.

TABLE 25

PERCENTAGE OF GROSS INCOME SPENT ON EACH CHILD BY MIDDLE INCOME[a]
PRAIRIE FAMILIES, EXCLUDING HOUSING AND CHILD CARE EXPENDITURES[b]

Age of Youngest Child	Percentage of Gross Income		
	First Child	Second Child	Third Child
1	6%	6%	6%
2	8	9	8
3	8	9	9
4	8	9	10
5	8	9	10
6	8	9	10
7	8	9	11
8	8	9	10
9	8	9	10
10	9	9	10
11	9	9	10
12	9	9	10
13	10	9	10
14	10	9	10
15	11	10	10[c]
16	12	11	10[c]
17	13	12[c]	11[d]
18	13	13[c]	12[d]
Average cost	9%	9%	10%

[a] Middle-income families include those families with gross incomes of $30,000 to $45,000 per year in 1988.
[b] Excludes increased spending on durable goods, such as vehicles, appliances, and furniture, due to the presence of children.
[c] First child left home.
[d] Second child left home.

TABLE 26

PERCENTAGE OF ANNUAL CHILD REARING COSTS, EXCLUDING HOUSING AND
CHILD CARE, BY CATEGORY OF SPENDING: MIDDLE INCOME PRAIRIE FAMILIES

Age of Youngest Child	Spending Category							
	Food at Home	Clothing	Utilities	Household Operation	Trans-portation	Health Care	Education Related	Miscl.
First Child								
1	61%	8%	22%	0%	0%	0%	5%	4%
2	51	6	15	0	11	0	5	12
3	55	9	15	0	9	0	4	8
4	58	11	14	0	8	0	5	4
5	60	12	13	0	7	0	6	2
6	62	13	12	0	5	1	7	0
7	63	13	11	0	5	2	7	0
8	62	12	10	0	5	2	8	1
9	61	11	9	2	5	3	9	0
10	60	11	8	3	6	3	10	0
11	58	10	8	4	7	3	10	0
12	56	10	7	5	8	3	11	0
13	52	13	7	5	9	3	11	0
14	49	16	7	5	10	2	11	0
15	46	18	7	5	11	2	11	0
16	43	20	6	5	12	2	11	1
17	40	21	6	5	13	1	11	3
18	38	21	6	4	14	1	11	5
Average cost								
	54%	13%	10%	2%	8%	2%	8%	2%
Second Child[a]								
1	64%	16%	12%	0%	0%	0%	0%	8%
2	49	12	14	0	0	0	0	25
3	51	17	13	0	0	0	0	19
4	55	22	12	0	0	0	0	11
5	61	26	10	0	0	0	0	3
6	63	27	8	0	0	0	0	3
7	65	27	7	0	0	1	0	0
8	65	25	6	0	0	2	2	0
9	65	23	5	0	0	3	3	1
10	66	21	5	0	0	3	5	0
11	66	18	4	1	0	4	7	0
12	66	16	4	2	0	3	9	0
13	66	13	5	3	0	3	11	0
14	66	11	5	3	0	3	13	0
15	61	13	5	3	2	2	14	0
16	56	17	5	3	4	2	14	0
17	41	20	6	5	13	1	11	3
18	39	21	7	4	14	1	10	4
Average cost								
	59%	19%	8%	1%	2%	1%	6%	4%

TABLE 26 (continued)

PERCENTAGE OF ANNUAL CHILD REARING COSTS, EXCLUDING HOUSING AND
CHILD CARE, BY CATEGORY OF SPENDING: MIDDLE INCOME PRAIRIE FAMILIES

Age of Youngest Child	Spending Category							
	Food at Home	Clothing	Utilities	Household Operation	Trans-portation	Health Care	Education Related	Miscl.
Third Child[a]								
1	47%	33%	6%	0%	0%	0%	0%	14%
2	31	26	7	0	0	0	0	36
3	35	35	7	0	0	0	0	23
4	40	41	5	0	0	0	0	14
5	45	46	4	0	0	0	0	5
6	50	47	2	0	0	0	0	1
7	53	45	2	0	0	0	0	0
8	56	41	1	0	0	2	0	0
9	60	37	1	0	0	3	0	0
10	63	32	1	0	0	3	0	1
11	66	27	1	0	0	4	2	0
12	68	22	2	0	0	4	4	0
13	68	17	2	1	0	4	7	1
14	69	13	2	2	0	4	10	0
15	62	13	5	3	2	2	13	0
16	57	15	5	3	4	2	14	0
17	44	19	7	4	13	1	10	2
18	42	20	7	4	14	1	10	2
Average cost								
	53%	29%	4%	1%	2%	2%	4%	6%

[a] Assumes children are spaced two years apart.

TABLE 27

AVERAGE PERCENTAGE OF GROSS INCOME SPENT BY MIDDLE INCOME[a] PRAIRIE FAMILIES FOR HOUSING EXPENDITURES OVER THE LIFE CYCLE

Housing Category	One-Child Family	Two-Child Family	Three-Child Family
Home owners	13%	12%	11%
Renters	18%	17%	16%

[a] Middle income families include those families with gross incomes of $30, 000 to $45,000 per year in 1988.

TABLE 28

PERCENTAGE OF GROSS INCOME SPENT BY MIDDLE INCOME PRAIRIE FAMILIES FOR CHILD CARE EXPENDITURES BY PARENTAL EMPLOYMENT STATUS

Age of Youngest Child	One Child		Two Children		Three Children	
	Both Parents Employed	One Parent Employed	Both Parents Employed	One Parent Employed	Both Parents Employed	One Parent Employed
1	4%	*	4%	1%	5%	1%
2	4	1	4	1	4	1
3	3	1	3	1	3	1
4	3	*	3	1	3	1
5	3	*	3	*	2	1
6	2	*	2	*	2	1
7	2	*	2	*	2	*
8	2	*	2	*	2	*
9	2	*	2	*	2	*
10	2	*	2	*	2	*
11	1	*	1	*	2	*
Average cost	3%	*	3%	*	3%	1%

* Less than 1% of gross income annually.

TABLE 29

PERCENTAGE OF GROSS INCOME SPENT BY MIDDLE INCOME[a] PRAIRIE FAMILIES
ON CHILD REARING COSTS INCLUDING HOUSING[b]
AND CHILD CARE—
HOME OWNERS & BOTH PARENTS EMPLOYED[c]

Age of Youngest Child	Percentage of Gross Income		
	One-Child Family	Two-Child Family	Three-Child Family
1	11%	20%	31%
2	13	23	32
3	12	22	32
4	12	22	33
5	12	22	32
6	11	21	33
7	11	21	34
8	11	22	33
9	11	22	34
10	12	22	34
11	11	22	35
12	10	21	34
13	11	22	36
14	11	23	37
15	12	25	24[d]
16	13	26	25[d]
17	14	13[d]	12[e]
18	14	14[d]	13[e]
Average cost	12%	20%[f]	28%[f]

[a] Middle income families include those families with incomes of $30,000 to $45,000 per year in 1988.
[b] 1% of gross income has been added to cover the cost of an additional room for home owners, add 1% gross income for the cost of an additional room for renters.
[c] Excludes increased spending on durable goods, such as vehicles, appliances, and furniture, due to the presence of children.
[d] First child left home.
[e] Second child left home.
[f] Averages include years prior to last child's birth when other children were present.

TABLE 30

PERCENTAGE OF GROSS INCOME SAVED BY MIDDLE INCOME PRAIRIE FAMILIES OF DIFFERENT COMPOSITION OVER THE LIFE CYCLE

Age of Adult Male	Childless Couple	Age of First Child	One - Child Family	Age of Second Child	Two - Child Family	Age of Third Child	Three - Child Family
28	11%						
29	10	1	15%				
30	10	2	9				
31	10	3	8	1	13%		
32	10	4	8	2	8		
33	10	5	9	3	8	1	14%
34	10	6	9	4	9	2	9
35	10	7	10	5	10	3	9
36	10	8	10	6	10	4	11
37	11	9	10	7	11	5	12
38	11	10	10	8	11	6	12
39	11	11	10	9	11	7	13
40	11	12	10	10	11	8	13
41	12	13	10	11	11	9	13
42	12	14	10	12	11	10	12
43	13	15	10	13	10	11	12
44	13	16	10	14	10	12	11
45	14	17	10	15	9	13	10
46	14	18	10	16	9	14	9
47	15			17	11	15	10
48	15			18	11	16	10
49	16					17	12
50	16					18	12
Average	12%		10%		10%[a]		11%[a]

[a] Averages include years prior to last child's birth when other children were present.

124

TABLE 31

PERCENTAGE OF GROSS INCOME SPENT ON EACH CHILD BY LOWER-MIDDLE INCOME[a] PRAIRIE FAMILIES, EXCLUDING HOUSING AND CHILD CARE EXPENDITURES[b]

Age of Youngest Child	Percentage of Gross Income		
	First Child	Second Child	Third Child
1	4%	4%	4%
2	6	7	6
3	6	7	7
4	6	7	8
5	6	7	9
6	6	7	9
7	6	7	9
8	6	7	9
9	6	7	9
10	6	7	8
11	7	7	8
12	7	7	8
13	7	7	8
14	7	7	8
15	8	7	7[c]
16	8	7	7[c]
17	9	9[c]	8[d]
18	9	9[c]	8[d]
Average cost	7%	7%	8%

[a] Lower-middle income families include those families with gross incomes of $15,000 to $30,000 per year in 1988.
[b] Excludes increased spending on durable goods, such as vehicles, appliances, and furniture, due to the presence of children.
[c] First child left home.
[d] Second child left home.

TABLE 32

PERCENTAGE OF ANNUAL CHILD REARING COSTS, EXCLUDING HOUSING AND CHILD CARE, BY CATEGORY OF SPENDING: LOWER-MIDDLE INCOME PRAIRIE FAMILIES

Age of Youngest Child	Spending Category							
	Food at Home	Clothing	Utilities	Household Operation	Trans-portation	Health Care	Education Related	Miscl.
First Child								
1	62%	11%	6%	2%	9%	0%	6%	4%
2	57	7	15	0	8	0	4	9
3	60	10	15	0	6	0	4	5
4	63	12	14	0	4	0	4	3
5	66	13	13	0	3	0	5	0
6	68	14	11	0	1	0	6	0
7	68	14	10	0	1	1	6	0
8	68	13	9	0	1	2	7	0
9	68	13	8	0	1	2	8	0
10	67	12	7	0	2	2	9	1
11	66	11	7	1	3	2	10	0
12	65	10	7	2	4	2	11	0
13	61	11	6	2	6	2	11	1
14	58	14	6	3	7	2	11	0
15	55	16	6	3	8	1	11	0
16	52	17	6	3	10	1	12	0
17	49	18	6	3	11	0	12	1
18	47	19	6	2	12	0	12	2
Average cost								
	61%	13%	9%	1%	5%	1%	8%	1%
Second Child[a]								
1	68%	25%	0%	0%	0%	0%	0%	7%
2	54	14	14	0	0	0	0	18
3	55	19	13	0	0	0	0	13
4	58	23	11	0	0	0	0	8
5	62	27	9	0	0	0	0	2
6	64	28	7	0	0	0	0	1
7	66	28	5	0	0	1	0	0
8	67	26	4	0	0	1	1	1
9	68	24	4	0	0	2	2	0
10	68	22	3	0	0	2	4	1
11	69	20	3	0	0	3	6	0
12	70	17	3	0	0	3	8	0
13	71	14	3	0	0	2	9	1
14	71	12	3	0	0	2	11	1
15	71	11	3	1	0	2	13	0
16	67	14	3	0	0	1	15	0
17	50	18	6	3	11	0	11	1
18	48	19	6	2	12	0	11	2
Average cost								
	64%	20%	6%	0%	1%	1%	5%	3%

TABLE 32 (continued)

PERCENTAGE OF ANNUAL CHILD REARING COSTS, EXCLUDING HOUSING AND CHILD CARE, BY CATEGORY OF SPENDING: LOWER-MIDDLE INCOME PRAIRIE FAMILIES

Age of Youngest Child	Food at Home	Clothing	Utilities	Household Operation	Trans-portation	Health Care	Education Related	Miscl.
Third Child[a]								
1	41%	46%	0%	0%	0%	0%	0%	13%
2	36	29	7	0	0	0	0	28
3	38	37	7	0	0	0	0	18
4	42	44	5	0	0	0	0	9
5	46	48	3	0	0	0	0	3
6	50	48	1	0	0	0	0	1
7	54	46	0	0	0	0	0	0
8	57	42	0	0	0	1	0	0
9	60	38	0	0	0	2	0	0
10	64	33	0	0	0	3	0	0
11	68	28	0	0	0	3	1	0
12	70	23	0	0	0	3	3	1
13	72	19	0	0	0	3	6	0
14	74	15	0	0	0	3	9	0
15	72	11	3	1	0	2	13	0
16	68	13	3	0	0	1	14	1
17	52	17	6	2	11	0	11	1
18	50	18	6	2	12	0	11	1
Average cost								
	56%	31%	2%	0%	1%	1%	4%	4%

[a] Assumes children are spaced two years apart.

TABLE 33

Average Percentage of Gross Income Spent by Lower-Middle Income[a] Prairie Families for Housing Expenditures over the Life Cycle

Housing Category	One-Child Family	Two-Child Family	Three-Child Family
Home owners	10%	9%	9%
Renters	17%	16%	15%

[a] Lower-middle income families include those families with gross incomes of $15, 000 to $30,000 per year in 1988.

TABLE 34

PERCENTAGE OF GROSS INCOME SPENT BY LOWER-MIDDLE INCOME PRAIRIE FAMILIES FOR CHILD CARE EXPENDITURES BY PARENTAL EMPLOYMENT STATUS

Age of Youngest Child	One Child		Two Children		Three Children	
	Both Parents Employed	One Parent Employed	Both Parents Employed	One Parent Employed	Both Parents Employed	One Parent Employed
1	4%	1%	4%	1%	5%	1%
2	4	1	4	1	4	1
3	3	1	3	1	3	*
4	3	*	3	*	3	*
5	2	*	2	*	2	*
6	2	*	2	*	2	*
7	2	*	2	*	2	*
8	2	*	2	*	2	*
9	1	*	1	*	1	*
10	1	*	1	*	1	*
11	1	*	1	*	1	*
Average cost	2%	*	2%	*	2%	*

* Less than 1% of gross income annually.

TABLE 35

PERCENTAGE OF GROSS INCOME SPENT BY LOWER-MIDDLE INCOME[a] PRAIRIE FAMILIES ON CHILD REARING COSTS INCLUDING HOUSING[b] AND CHILD CARE—
HOME OWNERS & BOTH PARENTS EMPLOYED[c]

Age of Youngest Child	Percentage of Gross Income		
	One-Child Family	Two-Child Family	Three-Child Family
1	9%	16%	25%
2	11	19	26
3	10	18	26
4	10	18	27
5	9	17	27
6	9	17	27
7	9	17	28
8	9	17	28
9	8	17	27
10	8	17	26
11	9	17	27
12	8	16	26
13	8	17	27
14	8	17	27
15	9	18	18[d]
16	9	18	18[d]
17	10	10[d]	9[e]
18	10	10[d]	9[e]
Average cost	9%	16%[f]	22%[f]

[a] Lower-middle income families include those families with incomes of $15,000 to $30,000 per year in 1988.
[b] 1% of gross income has been added to cover the cost of an additional room for home owners, add 1% gross income for the cost of an additional room for renters.
[c] Excludes increased spending on durable goods, such as vehicles, appliances, and furniture, due to the presence of children.
[d] First child left home.
[e] Second child left home.
[f] Averages include years prior to last child's birth when other children were present.

TABLE 36

PERCENTAGE OF GROSS INCOME SAVED BY LOWER-MIDDLE INCOME PRAIRIE FAMILIES OF DIFFERENT COMPOSITION OVER THE LIFE CYCLE

Age of Adult Male	Childless Couple	Age of First Child	One - Child Family	Age of Second Child	Two - Child Family	Age of Third Child	Three - Child Family
28	6%						
29	6	1	9%				
30	6	2	5				
31	6	3	5	1	8%		
32	6	4	5	2	5		
33	6	5	5	3	5	1	8%
34	6	6	5	4	5	2	5
35	6	7	6	5	6	3	6
36	6	8	6	6	6	4	6
37	6	9	6	7	6	5	7
38	6	10	6	8	7	6	7
39	7	11	6	9	7	7	8
40	7	12	6	10	7	8	8
41	7	13	6	11	7	9	8
42	7	14	6	12	6	10	7
43	8	15	6	13	6	11	7
44	8	16	6	14	6	12	6
45	8	17	6	15	6	13	6
46	9	18	6	16	5	14	5
47	9			17	7	15	6
48	9			18	7	16	6
49	10					17	7
50	10					18	7
Average	7%		6%		6%[a]		7%[a]

[a] Averages include years prior to last child's birth when other children were present.

TABLE 37

PERCENTAGE OF GROSS INCOME SPENT ON EACH CHILD BY UPPER-MIDDLE INCOME[a] ONTARIO FAMILIES, EXCLUDING HOUSING AND CHILD CARE EXPENDITURES[b]

Age of Youngest Child	Percentage of Gross Income		
	First Child	Second Child	Third Child
1	12%	7%	9%
2	11	6	8
3	11	8	9
4	10	9	10
5	9	9	11
6	9	9	12
7	9	10	12
8	9	10	12
9	10	11	12
10	10	11	13
11	11	11	13
12	12	11	13
13	13	11	13
14	14	11	12
15	15	13	11[c]
16	16	14	12[c]
17	17	15[c]	12[d]
18	18	16[c]	12[d]
Average cost	12%	11%	11%

[a] Upper-middle income families include those families with gross incomes of $45,000 to $100,000 per year in 1988.
[b] Excludes increased spending on durable goods, such as vehicles, appliances, and furniture, due to the presence of children.
[c] First child left home.
[d] Second child left home.

TABLE 38

PERCENTAGE OF ANNUAL CHILD REARING COSTS, EXCLUDING HOUSING AND CHILD CARE, BY CATEGORY OF SPENDING: UPPER-MIDDLE INCOME ONTARIO FAMILIES

Age of Youngest Child	Food at Home	Clothing	Utilities	Household Operation	Trans- portation	Health Care	Education Related	Miscl.
First Child								
1	29%	5%	17%	13%	16%	8%	9%	3%
2	33	5	18	7	19	4	11	3
3	36	7	17	4	19	1	13	3
4	42	9	16	4	14	1	12	2
5	47	10	15	5	9	1	10	3
6	51	11	14	6	5	2	9	2
7	52	11	13	7	3	2	8	4
8	52	10	12	8	2	3	7	6
9	52	9	12	9	3	3	7	5
10	51	8	11	9	4	4	8	5
11	49	8	10	9	6	4	8	6
12	45	10	9	9	8	4	9	6
13	42	12	9	9	11	4	9	4
14	39	14	8	8	13	4	10	4
15	36	15	8	8	16	3	11	3
16	34	16	7	7	18	3	12	3
17	32	17	7	7	20	3	12	3
18	29	18	7	7	22	3	13	1
Average cost	42%	11%	12%	8%	12%	3%	10%	4%
Second Child[a]								
1	34%	18%	36%	0%	0%	6%	0%	6%
2	31	20	35	0	0	2	6	6
3	39	24	24	0	0	0	9	4
4	47	26	19	0	0	0	5	3
5	53	28	16	0	0	0	2	1
6	57	28	14	0	0	0	0	1
7	58	26	12	2	0	0	0	2
8	59	23	10	3	0	1	0	4
9	59	20	9	5	0	2	0	5
10	60	17	9	6	0	3	0	5
11	60	15	8	7	0	3	0	7
12	60	12	8	7	0	4	3	6
13	59	10	8	8	0	4	6	5
14	59	8	8	8	0	4	9	4
15	52	10	7	7	5	3	13	3
16	46	12	6	6	10	3	16	1
17	34	16	7	6	20	3	12	2
18	32	17	7	6	22	2	13	1
Average cost	50%	18%	14%	4%	3%	2%	5%	4%

TABLE 38 (continued)

PERCENTAGE OF ANNUAL CHILD REARING COSTS, EXCLUDING HOUSING AND CHILD CARE, BY CATEGORY OF SPENDING: UPPER-MIDDLE INCOME ONTARIO FAMILIES

Age of Youngest Child	Spending Category							
	Food at Home	Clothing	Utilities	Household Operation	Trans- portation	Health Care	Education Related	Miscl.
Third Child[a]								
1	41%	30%	23%	0%	0%	1%	0%	5%
2	35	35	24	0	0	0	0	6
3	29	48	19	0	0	0	0	4
4	31	52	15	0	0	0	0	2
5	37	50	10	0	0	0	0	3
6	43	48	8	0	0	0	0	1
7	48	44	7	0	0	0	0	1
8	53	39	6	0	0	0	0	2
9	57	33	6	0	0	1	0	3
10	59	27	5	2	0	2	0	5
11	61	21	6	4	0	3	0	5
12	62	17	6	6	0	3	0	6
13	64	13	6	7	0	4	0	6
14	67	10	6	7	0	4	0	6
15	56	9	7	6	4	3	12	3
16	50	11	6	5	9	3	16	0
17	40	14	7	5	20	2	13	0
18	37	14	6	4	22	2	13	2
Average cost								
	48%	29%	10%	3%	3%	2%	3%	3%

[a] Assumes children are spaced two years apart.

TABLE 39

AVERAGE PERCENTAGE OF GROSS INCOME SPENT BY UPPER-MIDDLE INCOME[a] ONTARIO FAMILIES FOR HOUSING OVER THE LIFE CYCLE

Housing Category	One-Child Family	Two-Child Family	Three-Child Family
Home owners	17%	15%	13%
Renters	20%	19%	19%

[a] Upper-middle income families include those families with gross incomes of $45, 000 to $100,000 per year in 1988.

TABLE 40

PERCENTAGE OF GROSS INCOME SPENT BY UPPER-MIDDLE INCOME ONTARIO
FAMILIES FOR CHILD CARE EXPENDITURES BY PARENTAL EMPLOYMENT STATUS

Age of Youngest Child	One Child		Two Children		Three Children	
	Both Parents Employed	One Parent Employed	Both Parents Employed	One Parent Employed	Both Parents Employed	One Parent Employed
1	5%	*	5%	*	4%	*
2	4	*	4	*	3	*
3	4	*	3	*	2	*
4	3	*	2	*	2	*
5	2	*	2	*	2	*
6	2	*	2	*	1	*
7	2	*	1	*	1	*
8	2	*	1	*	1	*
9	2	*	1	*	1	*
10	1	*	1	*	1	*
11	1	*	1	*	1	*
Average cost	3%	*	2%	*	2%	*

* Less than 1% of gross income annually.

TABLE 41

PERCENTAGE OF GROSS INCOME SPENT BY UPPER-MIDDLE INCOME[a]
ONTARIO FAMILIES ON CHILD REARING COSTS INCLUDING HOUSING[b]
AND CHILD CARE—
HOME OWNERS & BOTH PARENTS EMPLOYED[c]

Age of Youngest Child	Percentage of Gross Income		
	One-Child Family	Two-Child Family	Three-Child Family
1	19%	27%	36%
2	17	24	36
3	17	24	37
4	15	24	36
5	13	24	39
6	13	24	39
7	13	25	41
8	13	25	42
9	14	27	43
10	13	28	45
11	14	29	46
12	14	29	46
13	15	30	49
14	16	31	50
15	17	34	30[d]
16	18	36	32[d]
17	19	17[d]	12[e]
18	20	18[d]	12[e]
Average cost	16%	26%[f]	34%[f]

[a] Upper-middle income families include those families with incomes of $45,000 to $100,000 per year in 1988.
[b] 2% of gross income has been added to cover the cost of an additional room for home owners, add 2% gross income for the cost of an additional room for renters.
[c] Excludes increased spending on durable goods, such as vehicles, appliances, and furniture, due to the presence of children.
[d] First child left home.
[e] Second child left home.
[f] Averages include years prior to last child's birth when other children were present.

TABLE 42

PERCENTAGE OF GROSS INCOME SAVED BY UPPER-MIDDLE INCOME ONTARIO FAMILIES OF DIFFERENT COMPOSITION OVER THE LIFE CYCLE

Age of Adult Male	Childless Couple	Age of First Child	One - Child Family	Age of Second Child	Two - Child Family	Age of Third Child	Three - Child Family
28	38%						
29	38	1	28%				
30	38	2	30				
31	39	3	33	1	27%		
32	39	4	34	2	31		
33	39	5	35	3	34	1	27%
34	40	6	36	4	36	2	28
35	40	7	36	5	36	3	28
36	41	8	36	6	36	4	29
37	41	9	36	7	36	5	28
38	41	10	35	8	35	6	28
39	42	11	35	9	34	7	27
40	42	12	35	10	33	8	26
41	43	13	34	11	32	9	25
42	43	14	34	12	31	10	24
43	44	15	33	13	29	11	23
44	44	16	33	14	28	12	21
45	45	17	32	15	27	13	20
46	45	18	31	16	25	14	19
47	45			17	33	15	27
48	46			18	32	16	26
49	46					17	33
50	47					18	33
Average	42%		34%		32%[a]		26%[a]

[a] Averages include years prior to last child's birth when other children were present.

TABLE 43

PERCENTAGE OF GROSS INCOME SPENT ON EACH CHILD BY MIDDLE INCOME[a] ONTARIO FAMILIES, EXCLUDING HOUSING AND CHILD CARE EXPENDITURES[b]

Age of Youngest Child	Percentage of Gross Income		
	First Child	Second Child	Third Child
1	11%	7%	8%
2	9	5	6
3	9	7	8
4	9	8	9
5	9	9	11
6	8	9	11
7	9	9	11
8	9	9	11
9	9	10	11
10	9	10	11
11	10	10	12
12	10	10	12
13	11	10	11
14	12	10	10
15	13	10	10[c]
16	13	11	10[c]
17	14	13[c]	12[d]
18	15	14[c]	13[d]
Average cost	11%	10%	10%

[a] Middle income families include those families with gross incomes of $30,000 to $45,000 per year in 1988.
[b] Excludes increased spending on durable goods, such as vehicles, appliances, and furniture, due to the presence of children.
[c] First child left home.
[d] Second child left home.

TABLE 44

PERCENTAGE OF ANNUAL CHILD REARING COSTS, EXCLUDING HOUSING AND CHILD CARE, BY CATEGORY OF SPENDING: MIDDLE INCOME ONTARIO FAMILIES

Age of Youngest Child	Food at Home	Clothing	Utilities	Household Operation	Trans-portation	Health Care	Education Related	Miscl.
First Child								
1	30%	5%	17%	10%	19%	7%	8%	4%
2	35	6	20	5	17	4	11	2
3	40	8	18	3	17	0	13	1
4	46	10	17	3	12	0	11	1
5	49	11	15	4	8	1	10	2
6	53	11	15	6	4	1	9	1
7	54	11	13	7	2	2	8	3
8	55	11	12	7	1	3	7	4
9	54	10	12	8	2	3	7	4
10	53	9	11	8	3	3	7	6
11	52	8	10	9	5	4	8	4
12	49	9	9	8	7	4	9	5
13	45	11	9	8	10	4	9	4
14	43	12	8	8	12	3	10	4
15	40	14	8	7	15	3	11	2
16	37	15	7	7	17	3	12	2
17	35	15	7	6	20	3	12	2
18	33	17	7	6	22	2	13	0
Average cost	45%	11%	12%	7%	11%	3%	10%	3%
Second Child[a]								
1	33%	17%	34%	0%	0%	6%	0%	10%
2	31	21	36	0	0	1	5	6
3	40	24	24	0	0	0	8	4
4	47	27	19	0	0	0	5	2
5	53	28	16	0	0	0	1	2
6	57	28	13	0	0	0	0	2
7	59	26	11	1	0	0	0	3
8	60	24	10	3	0	1	0	2
9	61	21	9	4	0	2	0	3
10	62	18	8	5	0	3	0	4
11	63	15	8	6	0	3	0	5
12	63	13	8	7	0	3	2	4
13	62	10	8	7	0	4	5	4
14	62	8	7	7	0	4	9	3
15	58	9	7	6	3	3	12	2
16	51	11	6	5	8	2	16	1
17	37	15	7	6	20	2	12	1
18	35	16	7	5	22	2	13	0
Average cost	52%	18%	13%	3%	3%	2%	5%	3%

TABLE 44 (continued)

PERCENTAGE OF ANNUAL CHILD REARING COSTS, EXCLUDING HOUSING AND
CHILD CARE, BY CATEGORY OF SPENDING: MIDDLE INCOME ONTARIO FAMILIES

Age of Youngest Child	Food at Home	Clothing	Utilities	Household Operation	Trans-portation	Health Care	Education Related	Miscl.
Third Child[a]								
1	26%	35%	25%	0%	0%	0%	0%	14%
2	28	39	27	0	0	0	0	6
3	27	50	20	0	0	0	0	3
4	31	52	15	0	0	0	0	2
5	37	50	10	0	0	0	0	3
6	43	48	8	0	0	0	0	1
7	48	44	6	0	0	0	0	2
8	54	39	6	0	0	0	0	1
9	58	34	5	0	0	0	0	3
10	60	27	5	2	0	1	0	5
11	63	22	5	4	0	2	0	4
12	65	17	5	5	0	3	0	5
13	67	13	6	6	0	3	0	5
14	70	10	6	6	0	4	0	4
15	61	8	7	6	2	3	12	1
16	54	9	6	5	8	2	16	0
17	39	14	7	5	20	2	12	1
18	36	15	7	5	22	2	13	0
Average cost	48%	29%	10%	2%	3%	1%	3%	3%

[a] Assumes children are spaced two years apart.

TABLE 45

AVERAGE PERCENTAGE OF GROSS INCOME SPENT BY MIDDLE INCOME[a] ONTARIO FAMILIES FOR HOUSING EXPENDITURES OVER THE LIFE CYCLE

Housing Category	One-Child Family	Two-Child Family	Three-Child Family
Home owners	14%	12%	10%
Renters	17%	17%	16%

[a] Middle income families include those families with gross incomes of $30, 000 to $45,000 per year in 1988.

142

Table 46

Percentage of Gross Income Spent by Middle Income Ontario Families for Child Care Expenditures by Parental Employment Status

Age of Youngest Child	One Child		Two Children		Three Children	
	Both Parents Employed	One Parent Employed	Both Parents Employed	One Parent Employed	Both Parents Employed	One Parent Employed
1	6%	1%	6%	1%	5%	1%
2	5	*	4	*	4	*
3	4	*	4	*	3	*
4	4	*	3	*	3	*
5	3	*	3	*	2	*
6	3	*	2	*	2	*
7	3	*	2	*	2	*
8	2	*	2	*	1	*
9	2	*	2	*	1	*
10	2	*	1	*	1	*
11	2	*	1	*	1	*
Average cost	3%	*	3%	*	2%	*

* Less than 1% of gross income annually.

TABLE 47

PERCENTAGE OF GROSS INCOME SPENT BY MIDDLE INCOME[a] ONTARIO FAMILIES ON CHILD REARING COSTS INCLUDING HOUSING[b] AND CHILD CARE – HOME OWNERS & BOTH PARENTS EMPLOYED[c]

Age of Youngest Child	Percentage of Gross Income		
	One-Child Family	Two-Child Family	Three-Child Family
1	19%	26%	35%
2	16	22	32
3	15	24	35
4	15	23	36
5	14	25	37
6	13	24	37
7	14	24	39
8	13	24	38
9	13	26	39
10	13	25	40
11	14	26	42
12	14	26	41
13	13	27	41
14	14	27	42
15	15	28	27[d]
16	15	30	28[d]
17	16	15[d]	14[e]
18	17	16[d]	15[e]
Average cost	15%	24%[f]	32%[f]

[a] Middle income families include those families with incomes of $30,000 to $45,000 per year in 1988.

[b] 2% of gross income has been added to cover the cost of an additional room for home owners, add 2% gross income for the cost of an additional room for renters.

[c] Excludes increased spending on durable goods, such as vehicles, appliances, and furniture, due to the presence of children.

[d] First child left home.

[e] Second child left home.

[f] Averages include years prior to last child's birth when other children were present.

TABLE 48

**PERCENTAGE OF GROSS INCOME SAVED BY MIDDLE INCOME
ONTARIO FAMILIES OF DIFFERENT COMPOSITION OVER THE LIFE CYCLE**

Age of Adult Male	Childless Couple	Age of First Child	One - Child Family	Age of Second Child	Two - Child Family	Age of Third Child	Three - Child Family
28	25%						
29	26	1	18%				
30	26	2	20				
31	26	3	22	1	17%		
32	26	4	23	2	20		
33	27	5	24	3	17	1	17%
34	27	6	24	4	18	2	18
35	27	7	24	5	18	3	18
36	28	8	24	6	18	4	18
37	28	9	24	7	18	5	18
38	28	10	24	8	18	6	18
39	29	11	23	9	17	7	17
40	29	12	23	10	16	8	16
41	30	13	23	11	16	9	16
42	30	14	22	12	15	10	15
43	30	15	22	13	14	11	14
44	31	16	21	14	13	12	13
45	31	17	21	15	12	13	12
46	32	18	21	16	12	14	12
47	32			17	18	15	18
48	32			18	16	16	16
49	33					17	22
50	33					18	22
Average	29%		22%		17%[a]		17%[a]

[a] Averages include years prior to last child's birth when other children were present.

TABLE 49

PERCENTAGE OF GROSS INCOME SPENT ON EACH CHILD BY LOWER-MIDDLE INCOME[a] ONTARIO FAMILIES, EXCLUDING HOUSING AND CHILD CARE EXPENDITURES[b]

Age of Youngest Child	Percentage of Gross Income		
	First Child	Second Child	Third Child
1	8%	6%	7%
2	7	4	6
3	7	5	7
4	7	6	8
5	6	7	9
6	6	7	9
7	6	7	9
8	7	7	9
9	7	8	9
10	7	8	9
11	7	7	9
12	7	7	9
13	7	7	9
14	8	7	8
15	8	7	7[c]
16	9	7	7[c]
17	9	9[c]	8[d]
18	10	9[c]	8[d]
Average cost	7%	7%	8%

[a] Lower-middle income families include those families with gross incomes of $15,000 to $30,000 per year in 1988.

[b] Excludes increased spending on durable goods, such as vehicles, appliances, and furniture, due to the presence of children.

[c] First child left home.

[d] Second child left home.

TABLE 50

PERCENTAGE OF ANNUAL CHILD REARING COSTS, EXCLUDING HOUSING AND CHILD CARE, BY CATEGORY OF SPENDING: LOWER-MIDDLE INCOME ONTARIO FAMILIES

Age of Youngest Child	Food at Home	Clothing	Utilities	Household Operation	Trans- portation	Health Care	Education Related	Miscl.
First Child								
1	36%	6%	21%	7%	16%	6%	4%	4%
2	39	6	22	3	15	3	10	2
3	44	9	19	0	15	0	12	1
4	51	11	18	0	9	0	10	1
5	57	12	16	1	4	0	9	1
6	61	13	15	3	0	0	8	0
7	62	13	13	4	0	1	7	0
8	62	12	12	5	0	2	6	1
9	62	11	11	5	0	2	6	3
10	62	10	11	6	0	3	7	1
11	62	9	10	6	0	3	7	3
12	60	8	9	6	3	3	8	3
13	56	9	9	6	6	3	9	2
14	53	10	8	6	10	3	10	0
15	50	12	7	5	13	2	11	0
16	46	12	7	5	16	2	12	0
17	43	13	6	4	19	2	12	1
18	40	13	6	3	22	1	13	2
Average cost								
	53%	11%	12%	4%	8%	2%	9%	1%
Second Child[a]								
1	40%	19%	33%	0%	0%	4%	0%	4%
2	30	23	39	0	0	0	4	4
3	40	26	25	0	0	0	7	2
4	48	28	19	0	0	0	3	2
5	54	29	15	0	0	0	1	1
6	58	29	12	0	0	0	0	1
7	62	27	10	0	0	0	0	1
8	64	25	9	0	0	0	0	2
9	66	22	8	2	0	1	0	1
10	67	20	7	3	0	2	0	1
11	69	17	7	3	0	2	0	2
12	70	14	7	4	0	2	1	2
13	70	11	6	4	0	3	4	2
14	70	9	6	4	0	3	7	1
15	70	7	6	4	0	2	11	0
16	64	8	5	3	4	2	15	0
17	45	12	6	4	19	2	13	0
18	41	13	6	3	22	1	13	1
Average cost								
	57%	19%	13%	2%	3%	1%	4%	2%

TABLE 50 (continued)

PERCENTAGE OF ANNUAL CHILD REARING COSTS, EXCLUDING
HOUSING AND CHILD CARE, BY CATEGORY OF SPENDING:
LOWER-MIDDLE INCOME ONTARIO FAMILIES

Age of Youngest Child	Food at Home	Clothing	Utilities	Household Operation	Trans-portation	Health Care	Education Related	Miscl.
Third Child[a]								
1	40%	33%	24%	0%	0%	0%	0%	3%
2	38	34	24	0	0	0	0	4
3	31	48	19	0	0	0	0	2
4	30	54	14	0	0	0	0	2
5	37	52	9	0	0	0	0	2
6	43	49	7	0	0	0	0	1
7	49	45	5	0	0	0	0	1
8	55	40	4	0	0	0	0	1
9	60	35	4	0	0	0	0	1
10	64	29	4	0	0	1	0	2
11	67	23	4	2	0	2	0	2
12	70	19	4	3	0	2	0	2
13	73	15	4	3	0	3	0	2
14	77	11	4	4	0	3	0	1
15	72	6	5	3	0	2	11	1
16	66	4	4	2	3	1	15	2
17	48	1	6	3	18	1	13	0
18	45	0	5	2	22	1	13	0
Average cost								
	54%	28%	8%	1%	2%	1%	3%	2%

[a] Assumes children are spaced two years apart.

TABLE 51

**AVERAGE PERCENTAGE OF GROSS INCOME SPENT BY LOWER-MIDDLE INCOME[a]
ONTARIO FAMILIES FOR HOUSING OVER THE LIFE CYCLE**

Housing Category	One-Child Family	Two-Child Family	Three-Child Family
Home owners	11%	9%	7%
Renters	14%	14%	13%

[a] Lower-middle income families include those families with gross incomes of $15, 000 to $30,000 per year in 1988.

TABLE 52

PERCENTAGE OF GROSS INCOME SPENT BY LOWER-MIDDLE INCOME ONTARIO
FAMILIES FOR CHILD CARE EXPENDITURES BY PARENTAL EMPLOYMENT STATUS

Age of Youngest Child	One Child Both Parents Employed	One Parent Employed	Two Children Both Parents Employed	One Parent Employed	Three Children Both Parents Employed	One Parent Employed
1	7%	1%	6%	1%	6%	1%
2	5	*	5	*	4	*
3	5	*	4	*	3	*
4	4	*	3	*	3	*
5	3	*	3	*	2	*
6	3	*	2	*	2	*
7	3	*	2	*	1	*
8	2	*	2	*	1	*
9	2	*	1	*	1	*
10	2	*	1	*	1	*
11	2	*	1	*	1	*
Average cost	3%	*	3%	*	2%	*

* Less than 1% of gross income annually.

TABLE 53

PERCENTAGE OF GROSS INCOME SPENT BY LOWER-MIDDLE INCOME[a]
ONTARIO FAMILIES ON CHILD REARING COSTS **INCLUDING** HOUSING[b]
AND CHILD CARE –
HOME OWNERS & BOTH PARENTS EMPLOYED[c]

Age of Youngest Child	Percentage of Gross Income		
	One-Child Family	Two-Child Family	Three-Child Family
1	16%	21%	27%
2	13	18	27
3	13	17	29
4	12	17	28
5	10	18	28
6	10	18	28
7	10	18	28
8	10	18	28
9	10	18	27
10	10	18	28
11	10	17	28
12	8	17	28
13	8	17	27
14	9	18	28
15	9	18	18[d]
16	10	19	18[d]
17	10	10[d]	9[e]
18	11	10[d]	9[e]
Average cost	11%	17%[f]	23%[f]

[a] Lower-middle income families include those families with gross incomes of $15,000 to $30,000 per year in 1988.
[b] 1% of gross income has been added to cover the cost of an additional room for home owners, add 1% gross income for the cost of an additional room for renters.
[c] Excludes increased spending on durable goods, such as vehicles, appliances, and furniture, due to the presence of children.
[d] First child left home.
[e] Second child left home.
[f] Averages include years prior to last child's birth when other children were present.

TABLE 54

PERCENTAGE OF GROSS INCOME SAVED BY LOWER-MIDDLE INCOME ONTARIO FAMILIES OF DIFFERENT COMPOSITION OVER THE LIFE CYCLE

Age of Adult Male	Childless Couple	Age of First Child	One - Child Family	Age of Second Child	Two - Child Family	Age of Third Child	Three - Child Family
28	15%						
29	15	1	10%				
30	16	2	12				
31	16	3	13	1	10%		
32	16	4	14	2	12		
33	16	5	14	3	13	1	10%
34	16	6	14	4	14	2	10
35	17	7	14	5	15	3	11
36	17	8	14	6	15	4	11
37	17	9	14	7	14	5	10
38	17	10	14	8	14	6	10
39	18	11	14	9	14	7	10
40	18	12	14	10	13	8	9
41	18	13	13	11	12	9	9
42	19	14	13	12	12	10	8
43	19	15	13	13	11	11	8
44	19	16	13	14	10	12	8
45	19	17	12	15	10	13	7
46	20	18	12	16	9	14	7
47	20			17	13	15	10
48	20			18	12	16	9
49	20					17	13
50	21					18	13
Average	18%		13%		12%[a]		10%[a]

[a] Averages include years prior to last child's birth when other children were present.

152

TABLE 55

PERCENTAGE OF GROSS INCOME SPENT ON EACH CHILD BY UPPER-MIDDLE INCOME[a] QUEBEC FAMILIES, EXCLUDING HOUSING AND CHILD CARE EXPENDITURES[b]

Age of Youngest Child	Percentage of Gross Income		
	First Child	Second Child	Third Child
1	5%	3%	3%
2	7	6	7
3	7	9	10
4	7	10	13
5	8	11	14
6	8	11	15
7	8	11	15
8	9	12	15
9	9	12	15
10	9	12	15
11	9	12	14
12	9	11	14
13	9	11	14
14	9	10	13
15	9	10	10[c]
16	10	10	10[c]
17	10	10[c]	9[d]
18	11	11[c]	10[d]
Average cost	9%	10%	12%

[a] Upper-middle income families include those families with gross incomes of $45,000 to $100,000 per year in 1988.
[b] Excludes increased spending on durable goods, such as vehicles, appliances, and furniture, due to the presence of children.
[c] First child left home.
[d] Second child left home.

TABLE 56

Percentage of Annual Child Rearing Costs, Excluding Housing and Child Care, by Category of Spending: Upper-Middle Income Quebec Families

Age of Youngest Child	Food at Home	Clothing	Utilities	Household Operation	Trans-portation	Health Care	Education Related	Miscl.
First Child								
1	59%	9%	22%	4%	6%	0%	0%	0%
2	64	10	14	1	7	0	0	4
3	62	12	13	0	3	0	0	10
4	64	13	13	0	0	0	0	10
5	65	13	12	0	0	1	3	6
6	66	13	11	1	0	2	4	3
7	67	13	11	2	0	2	6	0
8	66	12	11	2	0	2	7	0
9	66	11	10	2	0	2	8	1
10	67	11	10	2	0	2	9	0
11	67	10	10	2	0	1	9	1
12	68	9	10	2	1	1	10	0
13	67	8	10	1	5	0	10	0
14	65	6	9	1	9	0	10	0
15	62	8	8	0	12	0	10	0
16	57	11	8	0	16	0	9	0
17	53	13	7	0	19	0	8	0
18	49	15	6	0	22	0	8	0
Average cost	63%	11%	11%	1%	6%	1%	6%	2%
Second Child[a]								
1	55%	32%	12%	0%	0%	0%	0%	1%
2	52	22	11	0	0	0	0	15
3	47	21	9	0	0	0	0	23
4	50	22	8	0	0	0	0	20
5	53	22	8	0	0	2	0	15
6	58	22	8	0	0	3	0	9
7	62	21	8	0	0	3	1	6
8	64	20	8	0	0	4	3	1
9	66	18	8	1	0	3	4	0
10	67	16	7	1	0	3	5	1
11	68	14	7	1	0	3	6	1
12	70	12	7	1	0	2	7	1
13	72	10	7	1	0	2	8	0
14	75	9	7	0	0	1	8	0
15	76	7	7	0	1	0	9	0
16	73	5	7	0	7	0	8	0
17	55	11	7	0	18	0	8	1
18	51	14	6	0	21	0	8	0
Average cost	62%	17%	8%	0%	3%	1%	4%	5%

TABLE 56 (continued)

PERCENTAGE OF ANNUAL CHILD REARING COSTS, EXCLUDING HOUSING AND CHILD CARE, BY CATEGORY OF SPENDING: UPPER-MIDDLE INCOME QUEBEC FAMILIES

Age of Youngest Child	Spending Category							
	Food at Home	Clothing	Utilities	Household Operation	Trans-portation	Health Care	Education Related	Miscl.
Third Child[a]								
1	27%	63%	11%	0%	0%	0%	0%	0%
2	26	43	6	0	0	0	0	25
3	28	37	5	0	0	0	0	30
4	35	36	5	0	0	1	0	23
5	41	35	5	0	0	2	0	17
6	47	33	5	0	0	3	0	12
7	53	31	5	0	0	4	0	7
8	58	29	5	0	0	4	0	4
9	62	25	5	0	0	4	1	3
10	65	21	5	1	0	4	2	2
11	68	18	6	1	0	4	4	0
12	70	15	6	1	0	3	4	1
13	73	12	6	1	0	3	5	0
14	76	10	6	1	0	2	6	0
15	78	7	7	0	0	0	8	0
16	75	5	6	0	6	0	8	0
17	58	10	7	0	17	0	8	0
18	55	11	6	0	20	0	7	1
Average cost								
	55%	25%	6%	0%	2%	2%	3%	7%

[a] Assumes children are spaced two years apart.

TABLE 57

AVERAGE PERCENTAGE OF GROSS INCOME SPENT BY UPPER-MIDDLE INCOME[a] QUEBEC FAMILIES FOR HOUSING OVER THE LIFE CYCLE

Housing Category	One-Child Family	Two-Child Family	Three-Child Family
Home owners	9%	8%	8%
Renters	11%	11%	11%

[a] Upper-middle income families include those families with gross incomes of $45, 000 to $100,000 per year in 1988.

TABLE 58

PERCENTAGE OF GROSS INCOME SPENT BY UPPER-MIDDLE INCOME QUEBEC
FAMILIES FOR CHILD CARE EXPENDITURES BY PARENTAL EMPLOYMENT STATUS

Age of Youngest Child	One Child		Two Children		Three Children	
	Both Parents Employed	One Parent Employed	Both Parents Employed	One Parent Employed	Both Parents Employed	One Parent Employed
1	5%	1%	5%	1%	5%	1%
2	4	1	4	1	4	1
3	3	1	4	1	3	*
4	3	1	3	*	3	*
5	3	*	3	*	3	*
6	3	*	3	*	3	*
7	2	*	2	*	2	*
8	2	*	2	*	2	*
9	2	*	2	*	2	*
10	2	*	2	*	2	*
11	2	*	2	*	2	*
Average cost	3%	*	3%	*	3%	*

* Less than 1% of gross income annually.

TABLE 59

Percentage of Gross Income Spent by Upper-Middle Income[a] Quebec Families on Child Rearing Costs INCLUDING Housing[b] and Child Care –
HOME OWNERS & BOTH PARENTS EMPLOYED[c]

Age of Youngest Child	Percentage of Gross Income		
	One-Child Family	Two-Child Family	Three-Child Family
1	11%	17%	28%
2	12	19	32
3	11	23	35
4	11	23	39
5	12	24	40
6	12	25	42
7	11	24	41
8	12	25	41
9	12	25	41
10	12	25	40
11	12	25	39
12	10	22	37
13	10	22	37
14	10	22	37
15	10	22	22[d]
16	11	23	23[d]
17	11	11[d]	10[e]
18	12	12[d]	11[e]
Average cost	11%	21%[f]	30%[f]

[a] Upper-middle income families include those families with incomes of $45,000 to $100,000 per year in 1988.

[b] 1% of gross income has been added to cover the cost of an additional room for home owners, add 2% gross income for the cost of an additional room for renters.

[c] Excludes increased spending on durable goods, such as vehicles, appliances, and furniture, due to the presence of children.

[d] First child left home.

[e] Second child left home.

[f] Averages include years prior to last child's birth when other children were present.

TABLE 60

PERCENTAGE OF GROSS INCOME SAVED BY UPPER-MIDDLE INCOME QUEBEC FAMILIES OF DIFFERENT COMPOSITION OVER THE LIFE CYCLE

Age of Adult Male	Childless Couple	Age of First Child	One-Child Family	Age of Second Child	Two-Child Family	Age of Third Child	Three-Child Family
28	38%						
29	38	1	36%				
30	38	2	34				
31	38	3	34	1	34%		
32	38	4	35	2	33		
33	37	5	33	3	33	1	34%
34	37	6	35	4	34	2	33
35	37	7	35	5	35	3	34
36	37	8	35	6	35	4	35
37	37	9	35	7	35	5	35
38	37	10	34	8	34	6	35
39	37	11	34	9	34	7	35
40	37	12	34	10	33	8	35
41	37	13	33	11	33	9	34
42	37	14	33	12	32	10	33
43	37	15	33	13	31	11	32
44	37	16	32	14	31	12	31
45	37	17	32	15	30	13	30
46	37	18	31	16	29	14	28
47	37			17	32	15	30
48	38			18	32	16	29
49	38					17	33
50	38					18	32
Average	37%		34%		33%[a]		33%[a]

[a] Averages include years prior to last child's birth when other children were present.

TABLE 61

PERCENTAGE OF GROSS INCOME SPENT ON EACH CHILD BY MIDDLE INCOME[a] QUEBEC FAMILIES, EXCLUDING HOUSING AND CHILD CARE EXPENDITURES[b]

Age of Youngest Child	Percentage of Gross Income		
	First Child	Second Child	Third Child
1	5%	10%	5%
2	6	6	6
3	6	7	9
4	7	9	11
5	7	9	12
6	7	10	13
7	7	10	13
8	8	10	13
9	8	10	13
10	8	10	13
11	8	10	12
12	7	10	12
13	7	10	12
14	8	10	11
15	8	9	9[c]
16	8	9	8[c]
17	9	9[c]	8[d]
18	9	8[c]	8[d]
Average cost	7%	9%	10%

[a] Middle income families include those families with gross incomes of $30,000 to $45,000 per year in 1988.
[b] Excludes increased spending on durable goods, such as vehicles, appliances, and furniture, due to the presence of children.
[c] First child left home.
[d] Second child left home.

TABLE 62

PERCENTAGE OF ANNUAL CHILD REARING COSTS, EXCLUDING HOUSING AND
CHILD CARE, BY CATEGORY OF SPENDING: MIDDLE INCOME QUEBEC FAMILIES

Age of Youngest Child	Food at Home	Clothing	Utilities	Trans-portation	Education Related	Miscl.
First Child						
1	66%	16%	14%	0%	0%	4%
2	68	10	14	5	0	3
3	67	12	13	1	0	7
4	68	13	12	0	0	7
5	69	14	12	0	2	3
6	70	14	11	0	4	1
7	70	13	11	0	5	1
8	70	12	10	0	6	2
9	70	12	10	0	7	1
10	71	11	10	0	7	1
11	72	10	10	0	8	1
12	73	9	9	0	9	0
13	73	8	9	2	9	0
14	70	7	9	6	9	0
15	68	5	8	10	9	0
16	64	7	7	13	8	1
17	60	10	6	17	8	0
18	56	12	6	20	7	0
Average cost	68%	11%	10%	4%	5%	2%
Second Child[a]						
1	63%	9%	11%	0%	0%	17%
2	56	22	12	0	0	10
3	51	22	9	0	0	18
4	54	23	8	0	0	15
5	57	23	8	0	0	12
6	61	23	7	0	0	9
7	65	22	7	0	1	5
8	67	21	7	0	2	3
9	69	18	7	0	3	3
10	70	16	7	0	4	3
11	72	14	7	0	5	2
12	74	12	7	0	5	2
13	76	11	6	0	6	1
14	78	9	6	0	7	0
15	80	7	6	0	7	0
16	79	5	6	3	7	0
17	61	9	6	16	7	1
18	57	11	6	20	7	0
Average cost	56%	15%	7%	2%	3%	6%

TABLE 62 (continued)

PERCENTAGE OF ANNUAL CHILD REARING COSTS, EXCLUDING HOUSING AND CHILD CARE, BY CATEGORY OF SPENDING: MIDDLE INCOME QUEBEC FAMILIES

Age of Youngest Child	Food at Home	Clothing	Utilities	Trans-portation	Education Related	Miscl.
Third Child[a]						
1	44%	36%	17%	0%	0%	13%
2	31	45	7	1	0	17
3	32	39	5	0	0	24
4	39	38	5	0	0	18
5	44	37	4	0	0	15
6	50	35	4	0	0	11
7	55	33	4	0	0	8
8	61	30	4	0	0	5
9	65	26	4	0	0	5
10	68	22	4	0	1	5
11	71	18	5	0	2	4
12	74	15	5	0	3	3
13	77	12	5	0	4	2
14	80	10	5	0	4	1
15	81	7	6	0	7	0
16	81	5	5	3	6	0
17	64	7	6	15	7	1
18	60	9	5	19	6	1
Average cost						
	60%	24%	6%	2%	2%	7%

Spending Category

[a] Assumes children are spaced two years apart.

TABLE 63

**AVERAGE PERCENTAGE OF GROSS INCOME SPENT BY MIDDLE INCOME[a]
QUEBEC FAMILIES FOR HOUSING EXPENDITURES OVER THE LIFE CYCLE**

Housing Category	One-Child Family	Two-Child Family	Three-Child Family
Home owners	9%	8%	8%
Renters	11%	11%	11%

[a] Middle income families include those families with gross incomes of $30, 000 to $45,000 per year in 1988.

TABLE 64

PERCENTAGE OF GROSS INCOME SPENT BY MIDDLE INCOME QUEBEC FAMILIES FOR CHILD CARE EXPENDITURES BY PARENTAL EMPLOYMENT STATUS

Age of Youngest Child	One Child		Two Children		Three Children	
	Both Parents Employed	One Parent Employed	Both Parents Employed	One Parent Employed	Both Parents Employed	One Parent Employed
1	5%	1%	5%	1%	6%	1%
2	4	1	5	1	4	1
3	4	*	4	1	4	1
4	3	*	3	1	3	*
5	3	*	3	*	3	*
6	3	*	3	*	3	*
7	3	*	2	*	2	*
8	2	*	2	*	2	*
9	2	*	2	*	2	*
10	2	*	2	*	2	*
11	2	*	2	*	2	*
Average cost	2%	*	2%	*	2%	*

* Less than 1% of gross income annually.

TABLE 65

PERCENTAGE OF GROSS INCOME SPENT BY MIDDLE INCOME[a] QUEBEC FAMILIES
ON CHILD REARING COSTS INCLUDING HOUSING[b] AND CHILD CARE–
HOME OWNERS & BOTH PARENTS EMPLOYED[c]

Age of Youngest Child	Percentage of Gross Income		
	One-Child Family	Two-Child Family	Three-Child Family
1	11%	23%	28%
2	11	20	29
3	11	20	32
4	11	21	35
5	11	21	36
6	11	23	37
7	11	22	36
8	11	22	35
9	11	22	35
10	11	21	36
11	11	21	35
12	8	20	33
13	8	20	33
14	9	20	32
15	9	20	20[d]
16	9	20	18[d]
17	10	10[d]	9[e]
18	10	9[d]	9[e]
Average cost	10%	19%[f]	27%[f]

[a] Middle income families include those families with incomes of $30,000 to $45,000 per year in 1988.
[b] 1% of gross income has been added to cover the cost of an additional room for home owners, add 2% gross income for the cost of an additional room for renters.
[c] Excludes increased spending on durable goods, such as vehicles, appliances, and furniture, due to the presence of children.
[d] First child left home.
[e] Second child left home.
[f] Averages include years prior to last child's birth when other children were present.

TABLE 66

PERCENTAGE OF GROSS INCOME SAVED BY MIDDLE INCOME QUEBEC FAMILIES OF DIFFERENT COMPOSITION OVER THE LIFE CYCLE

Age of Adult Male	Childless Couple	Age of First Child	One - Child Family	Age of Second Child	Two - Child Family	Age of Third Child	Three - Child Family
28	26%						
29	26	1	24%				
30	26	2	23				
31	26	3	23	1	23%		
32	25	4	22	2	22		
33	25	5	22	3	22	1	23%
34	25	6	23	4	23	2	22
35	25	7	23	5	23	3	23
36	25	8	23	6	23	4	23
37	25	9	23	7	23	5	24
38	25	10	23	8	23	6	24
39	25	11	23	9	23	7	24
40	25	12	22	10	22	8	23
41	25	13	22	11	22	9	23
42	25	14	21	12	21	10	22
43	25	15	21	13	21	11	21
44	25	16	20	14	20	12	20
45	25	17	19	15	19	13	19
46	25	18	19	16	19	14	18
47	25			17	21	15	20
48	26			18	21	16	19
49	26					17	22
50	26					18	21
Average	25%		22%		22%[a]		22%[a]

[a] Averages include years prior to last child's birth when other children were present.

TABLE 67

PERCENTAGE OF GROSS INCOME SPENT ON EACH CHILD BY LOWER-MIDDLE INCOME[a] QUEBEC FAMILIES, EXCLUDING HOUSING AND CHILD CARE EXPENDITURES[b]

Age of Youngest Child	Percentage of Gross Income		
	First Child	Second Child	Third Child
1	4%	4%	3%
2	5	5	5
3	5	6	7
4	5	7	8
5	6	8	9
6	6	8	10
7	6	8	10
8	6	8	10
9	6	9	10
10	6	8	10
11	7	8	10
12	6	8	10
13	6	8	9
14	6	7	9
15	6	7	7[c]
16	6	7	7[c]
17	7	6[c]	6[d]
18	7	7[c]	6[d]
Average cost	6%	7%	8%

[a] Lower-middle income families include those families with gross incomes of $15,000 to $30,000 per year in 1988.

[b] Excludes increased spending on durable goods, such as vehicles, appliances, and furniture, due to the presence of children.

[c] First child left home.

[d] Second child left home.

TABLE 68

PERCENTAGE OF ANNUAL CHILD REARING COSTS, EXCLUDING HOUSING AND CHILD CARE, BY CATEGORY OF SPENDING: LOWER-MIDDLE INCOME QUEBEC FAMILIES

Age of Youngest Child	Spending Category							
	Food at Home	Clothing	Utilities	Household Operation	Trans-portation	Health Care	Education Related	Miscl.
First Child								
1	71%	9%	18%	2%	0%	0%	0%	0%
2	72	10	14	0	2	0	0	2
3	72	12	13	0	0	0	0	3
4	72	13	12	0	0	0	0	3
5	74	14	11	0	0	0	1	0
6	73	14	10	0	0	0	2	1
7	73	13	10	0	0	1	3	0
8	74	12	9	0	0	1	4	0
9	74	12	9	0	0	0	5	0
10	75	11	9	0	0	0	6	0
11	76	10	8	0	0	0	6	0
12	77	9	8	0	0	0	6	0
13	78	8	8	0	0	0	7	0
14	78	7	7	0	1	0	7	0
15	76	5	7	0	5	0	7	0
16	73	4	6	0	10	0	7	0
17	69	6	5	0	14	0	6	0
18	65	8	5	0	18	0	6	0
Average cost								
	73%	10%	9%	0%	3%	0%	4%	1%
Second Child[a]								
1	62%	22%	15%	0%	0%	0%	0%	1%
2	60	22	12	0	0	0	0	16
3	56	23	10	0	0	0	0	11
4	59	24	8	0	0	0	0	9
5	62	24	7	0	0	1	0	6
6	65	24	7	0	0	2	0	2
7	69	23	6	0	0	2	0	3
8	70	21	6	0	0	2	1	0
9	72	19	5	0	0	2	2	0
10	74	17	5	0	0	2	3	0
11	76	15	5	0	0	1	3	0
12	78	13	5	0	0	1	4	0
13	80	11	5	0	0	0	4	0
14	82	9	5	0	0	0	5	0
15	84	7	4	0	0	0	5	0
16	86	5	4	0	0	0	5	0
17	70	6	5	0	13	0	6	0
18	66	7	5	0	17	0	6	0
Average cost								
	71%	16%	7%	0%	2%	1%	2%	3%

TABLE 68 (continued)

PERCENTAGE OF ANNUAL CHILD REARING COSTS, EXCLUDING
HOUSING AND CHILD CARE, BY CATEGORY OF SPENDING:
LOWER-MIDDLE INCOME QUEBEC FAMILIES

Age of Youngest Child	Spending Category							
	Food at Home	Clothing	Utilities	Household Operation	Trans- portation	Health Care	Education Related	Miscl.
Third Child[a]								
1	37%	50%	13%	0%	0%	0%	0%	0%
2	36	45	8	0	0	0	0	11
3	36	42	6	0	0	0	0	16
4	42	41	5	0	0	0	0	12
5	48	39	4	0	0	2	0	7
6	53	37	3	0	0	2	0	5
7	58	34	3	0	0	3	0	2
8	64	31	3	0	0	3	0	0
9	68	27	3	0	0	3	0	0
10	72	23	3	0	0	3	0	0
11	75	19	3	0	0	2	1	0
12	78	15	3	0	0	2	2	0
13	81	12	3	0	0	1	2	1
14	84	10	3	0	0	0	3	0
15	85	7	4	0	0	0	5	0
16	87	5	4	0	0	0	5	0
17	72	4	5	0	12	0	6	1
18	68	6	4	0	16	0	5	1
Average cost								
	64%	25%	4%	0%	2%	1%	2%	3%

[a] Assumes children are spaced two years apart.

TABLE 69

AVERAGE PERCENTAGE OF GROSS INCOME SPENT BY LOWER-MIDDLE INCOME[a] QUEBEC FAMILIES FOR HOUSING OVER THE LIFE CYCLE

Housing Category	One-Child Family	Two-Child Family	Three-Child Family
Home owners	9%	8%	8%
Renters	12%	12%	12%

[a] Lower-middle income families include those families with gross incomes of $15,000 to $30,000 per year in 1988.

TABLE 70

PERCENTAGE OF GROSS INCOME SPENT BY LOWER-MIDDLE INCOME QUEBEC FAMILIES FOR CHILD CARE EXPENDITURES BY PARENTAL EMPLOYMENT STATUS

Age of Youngest Child	One Child		Two Children		Three Children	
	Both Parents Employed	One Parent Employed	Both Parents Employed	One Parent Employed	Both Parents Employed	One Parent Employed
1	5%	1%	5%	1%	5%	1%
2	4	1	4	1	4	1
3	3	1	3	1	3	1
4	3	1	3	*	3	*
5	3	*	2	*	2	*
6	2	*	2	*	2	*
7	2	*	2	*	2	*
8	2	*	2	*	2	*
9	2	*	2	*	2	*
10	1	*	1	*	1	*
11	1	*	1	*	1	*
Average cost	3%	*	2%	*	2%	*

* Less than 1% of gross income annually.

TABLE 71

PERCENTAGE OF GROSS INCOME SPENT BY LOWER-MIDDLE INCOME[a] QUEBEC FAMILIES ON CHILD REARING COSTS INCLUDING HOUSING[b] AND CHILD CARE–
HOME OWNERS & BOTH PARENTS EMPLOYED[c]

Age of Youngest Child	Percentage of Gross Income		
	One-Child Family	Two-Child Family	Three-Child Family
1	10%	16%	23%
2	10	16	25
3	9	17	27
4	9	18	28
5	10	18	28
6	9	18	29
7	9	18	31
8	9	18	29
9	9	20	29
10	8	17	28
11	9	17	28
12	7	16	26
13	7	16	26
14	7	15	26
15	7	16	15[d]
16	7	16	16[d]
17	8	7[d]	7[e]
18	8	8[d]	7[e]
Average cost	8%	15%[f]	22%[f]

[a] Lower-middle income families include those families with gross incomes of $15,000 to $30,000 per year in 1988.

[b] 1% of gross income has been added to cover the cost of an additional room for home owners, add 2% gross income for the cost of an additional room for renters.

[c] Excludes increased spending on durable goods, such as vehicles, appliances, and furniture, due to the presence of children.

[d] First child left home.

[e] Second child left home.

[f] Averages include years prior to last child's birth when other children were present.

TABLE 72

PERCENTAGE OF GROSS INCOME SAVED BY LOWER-MIDDLE INCOME QUEBEC FAMILIES OF DIFFERENT COMPOSITION OVER THE LIFE CYCLE

Age of Adult Male	Childless Couple	Age of First Child	One - Child Family	Age of Second Child	Two - Child Family	Age of Third Child	Three - Child Family
28	16%						
29	16	1	15%				
30	16	2	14				
31	16	3	14	1	14%		
32	16	4	14	2	13		
33	15	5	14	3	13	1	14%
34	15	6	14	4	14	2	13
35	15	7	14	5	14	3	14
36	15	8	14	6	14	4	14
37	15	9	14	7	14	5	14
38	15	10	14	8	14	6	14
39	15	11	14	9	14	7	14
40	15	12	13	10	13	8	14
41	15	13	13	11	13	9	14
42	15	14	13	12	13	10	13
43	15	15	13	13	12	11	13
44	15	16	13	14	12	12	12
45	15	17	13	15	11	13	11
46	15	18	12	16	11	14	11
47	16			17	13	15	12
48	16			18	12	16	11
49	16					17	13
50	16					18	13
Average	15%		14%		13%[a]		13%[a]

[a] Averages include years prior to last child's birth when other children were present.

TABLE 73

PERCENTAGE OF GROSS INCOME SPENT ON EACH CHILD BY UPPER-MIDDLE INCOME[a] ATLANTIC FAMILIES, EXCLUDING HOUSING AND CHILD CARE EXPENDITURES[b]

Age of Youngest Child	Percentage of Gross Income		
	First Child	Second Child	Third Child
1	8%	6%	9%
2	11	9	10
3	10	10	11
4	10	10	13
5	10	10	13
6	10	10	13
7	10	10	13
8	10	10	12
9	10	10	12
10	10	10	11
11	11	10	11
12	11	10	11
13	12	10	10
14	13	11	10
15	14	12	11[c]
16	15	13	12[c]
17	16	15[c]	13[d]
18	17	16[c]	13[d]
Average cost	12%	11%	12%

[a] Upper-middle income families include those families with gross incomes of $45,000 to $100,000 per year in 1988.
[b] Excludes increased spending on durable goods, such as vehicles, appliances, and furniture, due to the presence of children.
[c] First child left home.
[d] Second child left home.

TABLE 74

PERCENTAGE OF ANNUAL CHILD REARING COSTS, EXCLUDING HOUSING AND CHILD CARE, BY CATEGORY OF SPENDING: UPPER-MIDDLE INCOME ATLANTIC FAMILIES

Age of Youngest Child	Spending Category							
	Food at Home	Clothing	Utilities	Household Operation	Trans-portation	Health Care	Education Related	Miscl.
First Child								
1	63%	5%	10%	14%	0%	1%	8%	0%
2	51	6	15	15	6	0	6	1
3	55	9	13	14	4	0	5	0
4	55	10	12	14	4	0	4	1
5	56	11	12	13	4	0	4	0
6	57	12	11	13	4	0	4	0
7	57	12	10	12	5	0	4	0
8	56	11	9	12	7	0	5	0
9	55	11	8	12	9	0	5	0
10	53	10	8	12	11	0	6	0
11	52	9	7	12	13	0	7	0
12	50	8	7	13	15	0	8	0
13	47	6	6	13	17	0	9	2
14	45	5	6	13	18	1	10	2
15	42	4	5	13	20	1	10	5
16	40	3	5	13	21	1	11	6
17	37	2	5	13	22	1	11	9
18	36	2	4	13	23	1	12	9
Average cost	50%	8%	9%	13%	11%	0%	7%	2%
Second Child[a]								
1	62%	13%	18%	2%	0%	0%	5%	0%
2	54	14	17	5	0	0	0	10
3	63	21	13	4	0	0	0	0
4	62	25	10	3	0	0	0	0
5	62	27	9	2	0	0	0	0
6	63	28	7	2	0	0	0	0
7	64	28	6	2	0	0	0	0
8	65	26	6	3	0	0	0	0
9	66	25	5	4	0	0	0	0
10	68	22	5	5	0	0	0	0
11	68	20	5	6	0	0	1	0
12	68	17	4	8	0	0	3	0
13	64	13	4	9	4	0	6	0
14	60	10	3	10	9	0	8	0
15	56	7	2	11	13	0	10	1
16	52	5	2	11	17	0	13	0
17	40	2	4	13	22	1	11	7
18	38	1	4	13	23	1	11	9
Average cost	60%	17%	7%	6%	5%	0%	4%	2%

TABLE 74 (continued)

PERCENTAGE OF ANNUAL CHILD REARING COSTS, EXCLUDING HOUSING AND CHILD CARE, BY CATEGORY OF SPENDING: UPPER-MIDDLE INCOME ATLANTIC FAMILIES

Age of Youngest Child	Spending Category							
	Food at Home	Clothing	Utilities	Household Operation	Trans- portation	Health Care	Education Related	Miscl.
Third Child[a]								
1	62%	18%	20%	0%	0%	0%	0%	0%
2	58	28	14	0	0	0	0	0
3	52	40	8	0	0	0	0	0
4	50	45	5	0	0	0	0	0
5	50	47	3	0	0	0	0	0
6	51	47	2	0	0	0	0	0
7	53	45	2	0	0	0	0	0
8	56	42	2	0	0	0	0	0
9	60	38	2	0	0	0	0	0
10	64	34	2	0	0	0	0	0
11	69	29	2	0	0	0	0	0
12	72	24	2	1	0	0	0	1
13	74	19	2	4	0	0	0	1
14	75	15	1	6	0	0	3	0
15	59	7	2	10	12	0	10	0
16	55	5	1	11	16	0	12	0
17	43	2	4	12	22	0	10	7
18	41	1	3	13	23	0	10	9
Average cost								
	58%	27%	4%	3%	4%	0%	3%	1%

[a] Assumes children are spaced two years apart.

TABLE 75

AVERAGE PERCENTAGE OF GROSS INCOME SPENT BY UPPER-MIDDLE INCOME[a] ATLANTIC FAMILIES FOR HOUSING OVER THE LIFE CYCLE

Housing Category	One-Child Family	Two-Child Family	Three-Child Family
Home owners	10%	9%	8%
Renters	13%	13%	12%

[a] Upper-middle income families include those families with gross incomes of $45, 000 to $100,000 per year in 1988.

TABLE 76

PERCENTAGE OF GROSS INCOME SPENT BY UPPER-MIDDLE INCOME ATLANTIC FAMILIES FOR CHILD CARE EXPENDITURES BY PARENTAL EMPLOYMENT STATUS

Age of Youngest Child	One Child		Two Children		Three Children	
	Both Parents Employed	One Parent Employed	Both Parents Employed	One Parent Employed	Both Parents Employed	One Parent Employed
1	3%	*	3%	1%	3%	1%
2	3	*	3	*	3	*
3	3	*	3	*	2	*
4	3	*	2	*	2	*
5	2	*	2	*	2	*
6	2	*	2	*	2	*
7	2	*	2	*	2	*
8	2	*	2	*	2	*
9	2	*	2	*	2	*
10	2	*	2	*	2	*
11	2	*	2	*	2	*
Average cost	2%	*	2%	*	2%	*

* Less than 1% of gross income annually.

178

TABLE 77

PERCENTAGE OF GROSS INCOME SPENT BY UPPER-MIDDLE INCOME[a]
ATLANTIC FAMILIES ON CHILD REARING COSTS INCLUDING HOUSING[b]
AND CHILD CARE—
HOME OWNERS & BOTH PARENTS EMPLOYED[c]

| Age of Youngest Child | Percentage of Gross Income | | |
	One-Child Family	Two-Child Family	Three-Child Family
1	13%	23%	38%
2	16	26	39
3	15	27	39
4	15	26	41
5	14	26	41
6	14	26	41
7	14	26	42
8	14	26	41
9	14	27	42
10	14	27	42
11	15	28	43
12	13	27	43
13	14	28	44
14	15	30	46
15	16	32	30[d]
16	17	34	32[d]
17	18	17[d]	15[e]
18	19	18[d]	15[e]
Average cost	15%	25%[f]	34%[f]

[a] Upper-middle income families include those families with gross incomes of $45,000 to $100,000 per year in 1988.
[b] 2% of gross income has been added to cover the cost of an additional room for home owners, add 1% gross income for the cost of an additional room for renters.
[c] Excludes increased spending on durable goods, such as vehicles, appliances, and furniture, due to the presence of children.
[d] First child left home.
[e] Second child left home.
[f] Averages include years prior to last child's birth when other children were present.

Table 78

Percentage of Gross Income Saved by Upper-Middle Income Atlantic Families of Different Composition over the Life Cycle

Age of Adult Male	Childless Couple	Age of First Child	One - Child Family	Age of Second Child	Two - Child Family	Age of Third Child	Three - Child Family
28	41%						
29	41	1	44%				
30	42	2	39				
31	42	3	38	1	43%		
32	43	4	39	2	38		
33	43	5	39	3	38	1	43%
34	43	6	40	4	38	2	38
35	43	7	40	5	39	3	38
36	44	8	40	6	39	4	39
37	44	9	40	7	39	5	39
38	44	10	40	8	39	6	39
39	44	11	40	9	39	7	39
40	44	12	40	10	38	8	38
41	44	13	40	11	38	9	37
42	45	14	39	12	37	10	37
43	45	15	39	13	36	11	35
44	45	16	38	14	35	12	34
45	45	17	38	15	34	13	33
46	45	18	37	16	33	14	32
47	45			17	38	15	34
48	45			18	37	16	33
49	45					17	38
50	45					18	37
Average	44%		39%		38%[a]		37%[a]

[a] Averages include years prior to last child's birth when other children were present.

TABLE 79

PERCENTAGE OF GROSS INCOME SPENT ON EACH CHILD BY MIDDLE INCOME[a] ATLANTIC FAMILIES, EXCLUDING HOUSING AND CHILD CARE EXPENDITURES[b]

Age of Youngest Child	Percentage of Gross Income		
	First Child	Second Child	Third Child
1	9%	6%	10%
2	9	8	8
3	8	9	10
4	8	9	11
5	8	9	11
6	8	9	11
7	8	9	11
8	8	9	11
9	8	9	10
10	9	8	10
11	9	8	10
12	9	8	9
13	10	8	9
14	10	9	8
15	11	10	9[c]
16	11	10	10[c]
17	12	12[c]	10[d]
18	13	13[c]	11[d]
Average cost	9%	9%	10%

[a] Middle income families include those families with gross incomes of $30,000 to $45,000 per year in 1988.
[b] Excludes increased spending on durable goods, such as vehicles, appliances, and furniture, due to the presence of children.
[c] First child left home.
[d] Second child left home.

TABLE 80

PERCENTAGE OF ANNUAL CHILD REARING COSTS, EXCLUDING HOUSING AND CHILD CARE, BY CATEGORY OF SPENDING: MIDDLE INCOME ATLANTIC FAMILIES

Age of Youngest Child	Food at Home	Clothing	Utilities	Household Operation	Trans-portation	Education Related	Miscl.
First Child							
1	55%	4%	19%	10%	0%	5%	7%
2	56	6	15	14	3	5	1
3	60	9	13	13	1	4	0
4	60	11	12	12	1	3	1
5	61	13	11	12	1	3	0
6	62	13	10	11	1	3	0
7	61	13	9	11	3	3	0
8	61	13	8	11	4	4	0
9	60	12	7	11	6	4	0
10	58	11	6	11	9	5	0
11	56	10	6	11	11	6	0
12	55	8	5	12	13	7	0
13	53	7	5	12	16	8	0
14	50	6	4	12	18	9	1
15	48	5	4	12	19	9	3
16	45	4	4	12	21	10	4
17	43	3	3	13	22	10	6
18	40	2	3	13	24	11	7
Average cost							
	55%	8%	8%	12%	10%	6%	2%
Second Child[a]							
1	63%	11%	11%	1%	0%	1%	13%
2	67	15	16	3	0	0	0
3	65	22	11	2	0	0	0
4	64	26	9	1	0	0	0
5	64	28	7	1	0	0	0
6	64	29	6	0	0	0	1
7	66	29	5	1	0	0	0
8	67	28	4	1	0	0	0
9	68	26	4	2	0	0	0
10	70	24	3	3	0	0	0
11	72	21	3	5	0	0	0
12	72	18	2	6	0	2	0
13	70	15	2	7	1	5	0
14	66	11	1	8	6	7	1
15	62	8	1	9	11	9	0
16	58	6	0	10	15	11	0
17	44	2	3	12	22	10	7
18	42	2	3	12	24	11	6
Average cost							
	64%	18%	5%	5%	4%	3%	2%

Table 80 (continued)

Percentage of Annual Child Rearing Costs, Excluding Housing and Child Care, by Category of Spending: Middle Income Atlantic Families

Age of Youngest Child	Food at Home	Clothing	Utilities	Household Operation	Trans-portation	Education Related	Miscl.
Third Child[a]							
1	46%	14%	26%	0%	0%	0%	14%
2	58	29	12	0	0	0	1
3	53	41	6	0	0	0	0
4	50	47	4	0	0	0	0
5	49	49	2	0	0	0	0
6	50	49	1	0	0	0	0
7	53	47	0	0	0	0	0
8	56	43	0	0	0	0	1
9	60	39	0	0	0	0	1
10	65	35	0	0	0	0	0
11	70	30	0	0	0	0	0
12	74	25	0	0	0	0	1
13	78	21	0	2	0	0	0
14	79	16	0	4	0	2	0
15	64	8	0	9	10	9	0
16	60	5	0	10	14	11	0
17	48	2	2	12	22	9	5
18	45	2	2	12	24	10	5
Average cost							
	59%	28%	3%	3%	4%	2%	2%

[a] Assumes children are spaced two years apart.

TABLE 81

AVERAGE PERCENTAGE OF GROSS INCOME SPENT BY MIDDLE INCOME[a] ATLANTIC FAMILIES FOR HOUSING OVER THE LIFE CYCLE

Housing Category	One-Child Family	Two-Child Family	Three-Child Family
Home owners	8%	7%	6%
Renters	13%	12%	11%

[a] Middle income families include those families with gross incomes of $30, 000 to $45,000 per year in 1988.

184

TABLE 82

PERCENTAGE OF GROSS INCOME SPENT BY MIDDLE INCOME ATLANTIC FAMILIES FOR CHILD CARE EXPENDITURES BY PARENTAL EMPLOYMENT STATUS

Age of Youngest Child	One Child — Both Parents Employed	One Child — One Parent Employed	Two Children — Both Parents Employed	Two Children — One Parent Employed	Three Children — Both Parents Employed	Three Children — One Parent Employed
1	4%	1%	4%	1%	4%	1%
2	4	1	3	1	3	1
3	4	*	4	*	3	*
4	4	*	3	*	3	*
5	4	*	3	*	2	*
6	4	*	3	*	2	*
7	3	*	3	*	2	*
8	3	*	2	*	2	*
9	3	*	2	*	2	*
10	3	*	2	*	2	*
11	3	*	2	*	2	*
Average cost	4%	*	3%	*	2%	*

* Less than 1% of gross income annually.

TABLE 83

PERCENTAGE OF GROSS INCOME SPENT BY MIDDLE INCOME[a] ATLANTIC FAMILIES ON CHILD REARING COSTS INCLUDING HOUSING[b] AND CHILD CARE—
HOME OWNERS & BOTH PARENTS EMPLOYED[c]

Age of Youngest Child	Percentage of Gross Income		
	One-Child Family	Two-Child Family	Three-Child Family
1	15%	22%	37%
2	15	23	34
3	14	25	36
4	14	24	37
5	14	24	36
6	14	24	37
7	13	24	37
8	13	24	36
9	13	24	36
10	14	23	36
11	14	24	37
12	11	22	35
13	12	23	37
14	12	24	37
15	13	26	25[d]
16	13	27	27[d]
17	14	14[d]	12[e]
18	15	15[d]	13[e]
Average cost	14%	21%[f]	29%[f]

[a] Middle income families include those families with incomes of $30,000 to $45,000 per year in 1988.
[b] 2% of gross income has been added to cover the cost of an additional room for home owners, add 1% gross income for the cost of an additional room for renters.
[c] Excludes increased spending on durable goods, such as vehicles, appliances, and furniture, due to the presence of children.
[d] First child left home.
[e] Second child left home.
[f] Averages include years prior to last child's birth when other children were present.

TABLE 84

PERCENTAGE OF GROSS INCOME SAVED BY MIDDLE INCOME ATLANTIC FAMILIES OF DIFFERENT COMPOSITION OVER THE LIFE CYCLE

Age of Adult Male	Childless Couple	Age of First Child	One-Child Family	Age of Second Child	Two-Child Family	Age of Third Child	Three-Child Family
28	31%						
29	31	1	33%				
30	32	2	29				
31	32	3	29	1	32%		
32	32	4	29	2	28		
33	33	5	29	3	28	1	33%
34	33	6	30	4	28	2	29
35	33	7	30	5	29	3	28
36	33	8	30	6	29	4	29
37	33	9	30	7	29	5	29
38	34	10	30	8	29	6	29
39	34	11	30	9	29	7	29
40	34	12	30	10	29	8	28
41	34	13	30	11	28	9	28
42	34	14	29	12	27	10	27
43	34	15	29	13	27	11	26
44	34	16	29	14	26	12	25
45	34	17	28	15	25	13	24
46	34	18	28	16	24	14	23
47	34			17	28	15	25
48	34			18	28	16	24
49	34					17	28
50	34					18	28
Average	33%		28%		28%[a]		28%[a]

[a] Averages include years prior to last child's birth when other children were present.

TABLE 85

PERCENTAGE OF GROSS INCOME SPENT ON EACH CHILD BY LOWER-MIDDLE INCOME[a] ATLANTIC FAMILIES, EXCLUDING HOUSING AND CHILD CARE EXPENDITURES[b]

Age of Youngest Child	Percentage of Gross Income		
	First Child	Second Child	Third Child
1	7%	5%	7%
2	7	6	7
3	6	7	8
4	7	7	9
5	7	7	9
6	6	7	10
7	6	7	10
8	6	7	9
9	6	7	9
10	7	7	8
11	7	7	8
12	7	7	7
13	7	6	7
14	8	7	7
15	8	7	7[c]
16	8	7	7[c]
17	9	8[c]	8[d]
18	9	9[c]	8[d]
Average cost	7%	7%	8%

[a] Lower-middle income families include those families with gross incomes of $15,000 to $30,000 per year in 1988.
[b] Excludes increased spending on durable goods, such as vehicles, appliances, and furniture, due to the presence of children.
[c] First child left home.
[d] Second child left home.

TABLE 86

PERCENTAGE OF ANNUAL CHILD REARING COSTS, EXCLUDING
HOUSING AND CHILD CARE, BY CATEGORY OF SPENDING:
LOWER-MIDDLE INCOME ATLANTIC FAMILIES

Age of Youngest Child	Spending Category							
	Food at Home	Clothing	Utilities	Household Operation	Trans-portation	Health Care	Education Related	Miscl.
First Child								
1	63%	4%	20%	8%	0%	0%	4%	1%
2	63	7	14	12	0	0	4	0
3	65	10	11	10	0	0	3	1
4	65	13	10	10	0	0	2	0
5	66	14	9	9	0	0	2	0
6	67	15	8	9	0	0	2	0
7	68	15	7	9	0	0	2	0
8	68	14	6	9	0	0	3	0
9	67	14	5	9	3	0	3	0
10	65	12	4	9	5	0	4	1
11	63	11	3	9	8	0	5	1
12	61	10	3	10	10	0	6	0
13	59	8	2	10	13	0	7	1
14	57	7	2	11	16	0	7	0
15	55	5	2	11	18	0	8	1
16	53	4	1	12	20	0	9	1
17	50	3	1	12	22	0	9	3
18	48	2	0	12	24	0	10	4
Average cost								
	61%	9%	6%	10%	8%	0%	5%	1%
Second Child[a]								
1	71%	11%	18%	0%	0%	0%	0%	0%
2	70	16	14	0	0	0	0	0
3	67	23	9	0	0	0	0	1
4	66	28	7	0	0	0	0	0
5	65	30	5	0	0	0	0	0
6	66	31	4	0	0	0	0	0
7	67	31	3	0	0	0	0	0
8	69	30	2	0	0	0	0	0
9	71	28	1	0	0	0	0	0
10	73	26	0	1	0	0	0	0
11	75	23	0	2	0	0	0	0
12	76	20	0	3	0	0	1	0
13	76	16	0	5	0	0	3	0
14	74	13	0	6	2	0	5	0
15	69	9	0	7	7	0	7	1
16	64	6	0	8	12	0	9	1
17	52	3	0	12	22	0	9	2
18	49	2	0	12	24	0	10	3
Average cost								
	68%	19%	4%	3%	4%	0%	2%	0%

TABLE 86 (continued)

PERCENTAGE OF ANNUAL CHILD REARING COSTS, EXCLUDING HOUSING AND CHILD CARE, BY CATEGORY OF SPENDING: LOWER-MIDDLE INCOME ATLANTIC FAMILIES

Age of Youngest Child	Food at Home	Clothing	Utilities	Household Operation	Trans-portation	Health Care	Education Related	Miscl.
Third Child[a]								
1	55%	16%	29%	0%	0%	0%	0%	0%
2	59	31	10	0	0	0	0	0
3	52	43	4	0	0	0	0	1
4	49	49	1	0	0	0	0	1
5	49	51	0	0	0	0	0	0
6	49	51	0	0	0	0	0	0
7	52	48	0	0	0	0	0	0
8	55	45	0	0	0	0	0	0
9	59	41	0	0	0	0	0	0
10	64	36	0	0	0	0	0	0
11	69	31	0	0	0	0	0	0
12	74	26	0	0	0	0	0	0
13	78	22	0	0	0	0	0	0
14	82	17	0	1	0	0	0	0
15	71	9	0	7	7	0	7	0
16	66	6	0	8	12	0	9	0
17	54	3	0	11	22	0	9	1
18	52	2	0	11	23	0	9	3
Average cost								
	61%	29%	2%	2%	4%	0%	2%	0%

[a] Assumes children are spaced two years apart.

TABLE 87

AVERAGE PERCENTAGE OF GROSS INCOME SPENT BY LOWER-MIDDLE INCOME[a] ATLANTIC FAMILIES FOR HOUSING OVER THE LIFE CYCLE

Housing Category	One-Child Family	Two-Child Family	Three-Child Family
Home owners	6%	5%	4%
Renters	12%	11%	10%

[a] Lower-middle income families include those families with gross incomes of $15, 000 to $30,000 per year in 1988.

TABLE 88

PERCENTAGE OF GROSS INCOME SPENT BY LOWER-MIDDLE INCOME ATLANTIC FAMILIES FOR CHILD CARE EXPENDITURES BY PARENTAL EMPLOYMENT STATUS

Age of Youngest Child	One Child		Two Children		Three Children	
	Both Parents Employed	One Parent Employed	Both Parents Employed	One Parent Employed	Both Parents Employed	One Parent Employed
1	5%	1%	4%	1%	4%	1%
2	4	1	4	1	4	1
3	3	*	3	1	3	1
4	3	*	3	*	3	*
5	3	*	3	*	2	*
6	3	*	2	*	2	*
7	3	*	2	*	2	*
8	2	*	2	*	2	*
9	2	*	2	*	2	*
10	2	*	2	*	2	*
11	2	*	2	*	2	*
Average cost	3%	*	3%	*	3%	*

* Less than 1% of gross income annually.

Table 89

Percentage of Gross Income Spent by Lower-Middle Income[a] Atlantic Families on Child Rearing Costs INCLUDING Housing[b] and Child Care – HOME OWNERS & BOTH PARENTS EMPLOYED[c]

Age of Youngest Child	Percentage of Gross Income		
	One-Child Family	Two-Child Family	Three-Child Family
1	13%	17%	28%
2	12	19	27
3	10	19	27
4	11	18	28
5	11	18	27
6	10	17	29
7	10	17	29
8	9	18	28
9	9	18	28
10	10	18	28
11	10	18	27
12	8	17	25
13	8	16	26
14	9	17	26
15	9	18	17[d]
16	9	18	18[d]
17	10	9[d]	9[e]
18	10	10[d]	9[e]
Average cost	10%	16%[f]	23%[f]

[a] Lower-middle income families include those families with incomes of $15,000 to $30,000 per year in 1988.

[b] 1% of gross income has been added to cover the cost of an additional room for home owners, add 1% gross income for the cost of an additional room for renters.

[c] Excludes increased spending on durable goods, such as vehicles, appliances, and furniture, due to the presence of children.

[d] First child left home.

[e] Second child left home.

[f] Averages include years prior to last child's birth when other children were present.

TABLE 90

PERCENTAGE OF GROSS INCOME SAVED BY LOWER-MIDDLE INCOME ATLANTIC FAMILIES OF DIFFERENT COMPOSITION OVER THE LIFE CYCLE

Age of Adult Male	Childless Couple	Age of First Child	One - Child Family	Age of Second Child	Two - Child Family	Age of Third Child	Three - Child Family
28	21%						
29	22	1	23%				
30	22	2	20				
31	22	3	20	1	23%		
32	23	4	20	2	19		
33	23	5	20	3	19	1	23%
34	23	6	21	4	20	2	20
35	23	7	21	5	20	3	20
36	23	8	21	6	20	4	20
37	24	9	21	7	20	5	20
38	24	10	21	8	20	6	20
39	24	11	21	9	20	7	20
40	24	12	21	10	20	8	20
41	24	13	21	11	19	9	19
42	24	14	20	12	19	10	19
43	24	15	20	13	18	11	18
44	24	16	20	14	18	12	17
45	24	17	19	15	17	13	16
46	24	18	19	16	17	14	15
47	24			17	19	15	17
48	24			18	19	16	17
49	24					17	19
50	24					18	19
Average	23%		21%		19%[a]		19%[a]

[a] Averages include years prior to last child's birth when other children were present.

APPENDIX A

DETAILED METHODOLOGY DESCRIPTION

The empirical model used in this study incorporates both continuous measures of adult equivalence and a flexible functional form. A revealed preference approach using continuous household size and structural variables is adopted. Although revealed preference is a common approach for deriving equivalency measures found in the consumer demand literature,[1] few studies also incorporate a continuous (versus stepwise discrete) approach to measure the effects of family size and structure on spending behaviour.[2] Friedman (1957) first developed the concept of a continuous equivalence scale measure. Its strengths include continuity over size or age range measures (i.e., scales do not jump between adjacent age categories) and fewer required parameters for estimation. No studies in the consumer demand literature whose purpose is to explicitly measure the costs of raising children have used continuous scales.

The literature regarding the costs of raising children is replete with examples of studies which incorporate econometric models that *a priori* restrict estimated parameter values to be consistent with postulates of economic theory. For example, many expenditure allocation models assume functions homogeneous of degree one in income and family size (see for example Prais and Houthakker 1955). However, it can be demonstrated that the assumption of homogeneity can generate nonsensical results when applied to actual behaviour and that homogeneity, coupled with an equivalence scale specification, implies constant returns to scale. Numerous illustrations can be cited to refute the restriction that household composition changes yield constant returns to scale. The purchase of food in larger quantities sold at lower per unit prices and the reuse of clothing are standard examples of economies of scale which often occur upon the addition of a family member.

The present study incorporates a model which assures the theoretical restrictions of adding-up while allowing for nonhomogeneous demand functions and economies of scale. Thus, the model provides an effective balance between the concern for theoretical plausibility and the practical need to explain variance in the data.

One of the earliest authors to examine the influence of family composition on consumption was Earnst Engel (1895). Engel's work (and the work of many authors to follow) entailed normalizing the consumption of each family member relative to that of a base member. This in turn allowed him to compare standards of living across families by expressing total consumption of each as equivalent to a particular type of individual. For example, Engel used an infant (less than one year old) male child as the base unit in his early studies of food consumption and expressed all other individuals' consumption as the number of infant male equivalent units.

Later expenditure studies incorporated variants of the Engel equivalence scales by using the consumption of a particular type of adult or family unit as numeraire. However, in order to identify the omitted expenditure category using specific income scales, many such studies impose homogeneity and include a household equivalence measure calculated as the sum of adult equivalence scales in their expenditure models. Taken together these two constraints imply that there is 1) no interaction between size and family composition (thereby measuring only average rather than marginal effects of the addition) and 2) constant returns to scale. The isoprop model used by Espenshade (1984) is an example of this approach applied to the cost of raising children.

The economic model used in this analysis is the multinomial logit[3] budget allocation model (MLBAM) developed by Tyrrell in 1979. The MLBAM is expressed in the logistic form of the budget shares:

$$w_i = \frac{e^{f_i(M, P_1,...,P_n,Z,X)}}{\sum\limits_{j=1}^{n} e^{f_j(M,P_1,...,P_n,Z,X)}}, \qquad \text{for } (i,j=1,...n), \tag{1}$$

where:

w_i = the budget share of good i (and represents the probability that a given proportion of the budget is allocated to good i),

M = income (total expenditure),

P_k = the price of the kth good,

Z = a vector of family size and composition terms,

X = a vector of demographic characteristics, and

$f_i()$ = a function assumed linear in the unknown parameters.

Since the model is specified in terms of budget shares, the adding-up property is assured.

Data in this research are a cross-sectional sample of families; therefore, prices are assumed constant, and drop out of equation (1) such that:

$$w_i = \frac{e^{f_i(M,Z,X)}}{\sum\limits_{j=1}^{n} e^{f_j(M,Z,X)}}.$$ (2)

MLBAM also incorporates a continuous equivalence scale which varies with age in order to capture the effects of Z, household size and composition (age of family members). Departing from the usual method of specifying a separate equivalence coefficient for each age-sex group and adding these together to get the equivalence scale, the MLBAM follows Forsyth (1960) and specifies equivalent family size as the product of household size and composition variables for each good:

$$S_i = S\theta_i,$$ (3)

where:

S_i = equivalent family size with respect to good i,
S = actual family size, and
θ_i = a household composition term specific to good i.

The standard household is then defined by $\theta_i = 1$ and $S_i = S$. MLBAM also distinguishes between size effects — the effects on consumption due to the addition of a family member regardless of the type of person (e.g., the increase in the demand for necessities like food and clothing) — and composition effects — the effects on consumption due to the addition of a specific type of family member (e.g., the purchase of a crib for an infant). The model was formulated to examine these effects separately by taking the logarithm of equation (3).

The family composition function θ_i is specified so that $\ln\theta_i$ is linear in parameters:

$$\theta_i = e^{\sum\limits_{s=1}^{S} g_{is},}$$ (4)

where:

g_{is} = a transformation of the Sth family member's age.

Following Buse and Salathe (1978) and Blokland (1976), the MLBAM g_{is} are specified to be continuous functions, in the form of cubic polynomials in the sth family member's age:

$$g_{is} = c_{i0} + c_{i1}AGE_s + c_{i2}(AGE_s)^2 + a_{i3}(AGE_s)^3. \tag{5}$$

The definition of a standard consumer or family requires that for a certain age, equation (5) is normalized at zero, which is not possible to do directly. Instead, equation (5) is approximated using Lagrangian interpolation polynomials (LIP) first suggested by Almon (1965).[4] This technique transforms equation (5) into a linear combination of LIPs whose coefficients will approximate the values of equation (5). The LIPs are specified in terms of deviations around the four reference ages. The LIPs have the form:

$$L_1(a_s) = \frac{(a_s - a_2)(a_s - a_3)(a_s - a_4)}{(a_1 - a_2)(a_1 - a_3)(a_1 - a_4)}, \tag{5a}$$

$$L_2(a_s) = \frac{(a_s - a_1)(a_s - a_3)(a_s - a_4)}{(a_2 - a_1)(a_2 - a_3)(a_2 - a_4)}, \tag{5b}$$

$$L_3(a_s) = \frac{(a_s - a_1)(a_s - a_2)(a_s - a_4)}{(a_3 - a_1)(a_3 - a_2)(a_3 - a_4)}, \tag{5c}$$

$$L_4(a_s) = \frac{(a_s - a_1)(a_s - a_2)(a_s - a_3)}{(a_4 - a_1)(a_4 - a_2)(a_4 - a_3)}, \tag{5d}$$

where:

$a_s = 1n(\text{age of person } s)$
$a_1 = 1n(1),$
$a_2 + 1n(14),$
$a_3 = 1n(20),$
$a_4 = 1n(64), and$
$L_i = $ the ith LIP.

The LIP functions have the feature that if one of the reference ages is the person's actual age, the LIP corresponding to that reference age is equal to one while all the other LIPs equal zero. By taking the natural log of a family member's age, the estimated LIP parameters minimize the effects that higher ages would otherwise have on consumption in a linear specification.

Thus, the g_{is} function is written as:

$$g_{is} = \sum_{r=1}^{4} L_r(a_s).$$

(6)

Substitution of equation (6) into (4) and (4) into (3) gives a complete specification for the function f_i:

$$
\begin{aligned}
f_i(M,S_i,X) = &B_{i0} + B_{i1}ln(M) + B_{i2}ln(S) + B_{i31}[L_1(AGE_m) + \\
&L_1(AGE_f)] + B_{i32}[L_2(AGE_m) + L_2(AGE_f)] + B_{i33}[L_3(AGE_m) + \\
&L_3(AGE_f)] + B_{i34}[L_4(AGE_m) + L_4(AGE_f)] + B_{i35} \sum_{k=1}^{K} L_1(AGE_k) + \\
&B_{i36} \sum_{k=1}^{K} L_2(AGE_k) + B_{i37} \sum_{k=1}^{K} L_3(AGE_k) + B_{i38} \sum_{k=1}^{K} L_4(AGE_k) + \\
&\sum_{d=1}^{D} B_{i4d}X_d,
\end{aligned}
$$

(7)

where:

B_i = estimated coefficient
age_m = age of the adult male,
age_f = age of the adult female,
age_k = age of child k,
K = total number of children in the family ($K + 2 = S$), and
D = total number of demographic characteristics.

The standard consumer is defined to be a couple aged 20. Thus, the constraint is:

$$B_{i33} = 0.$$

(8)

In their study of equivalence scales using a human developmental approach, Tedford, Capps and Havlicek (1986) found that demographic characteristics, X, regarding whether 1) the family lived in a rural or urban area, 2) the household manager was college educated, and 3) the household manager was employed, influenced food expenditures. We include the same taste shifters in our specification.

The estimating equation then is:

$$w_i = \frac{e^{f_i(M,S,L_h,X)}}{\sum\limits_{j=1}^{n} e^{f_j(M,S,L_h,X)}} \quad , \qquad (h = 1, ...,8) \qquad (9)$$

where:

L = vector of family composition terms

with the f_i function specified in the form of equation (7). The model is estimated using an iterative Newton-Raphson (maximum likelihood) procedure. Identification of the system is achieved by setting the parameters of one equation equal to zero. Results are thus interpreted as being compared to the omitted category. Expenditures for other goods is the excluded equation.

The effect on total consumption of adding a specific person to a particular family type is measured as an arc elasticity, from which marginal expenditure estimates may be derived. This measure is closely related to the adult equivalent scale approach, however, normalization is defined to be the characteristics of the family before the addition of the marginal member. The arc elasticity is expressed as:

$$\eta_{is} = \frac{\delta Q_i}{\delta S} \frac{S}{Q_i} = \frac{w_i(S) - w_i(S\text{-}1)}{w_i(S) + w_i(S\text{-}1)} \quad (2S\text{-}1), \quad \text{for } (i=1, ...n) \qquad (10)$$

where:

Q_i = quantity of the ith good,
S = household size after the addition,
$w_i(S\text{-}1)$ = budget share before the particular addition,
$w_i(S)$ = budget share after the addition,
$S = [(S) = (S\text{-}1)]/2$, and
$Q_i = [w_i(S) + w_i(S\text{-}1)]/2$.

To summarize then, the MLBAM model satisfies the Engel and Cournot aggregation constraints (it can also be constrained locally to satisfy homogeneity and Slutsky symmetry conditions). It relates commodity expenditures to a nonhomogeneous function of total expenditures and household size, thereby allowing for economies and diseconomies of scale. In addition, it allows examination of the effect on commodity expenditures of adding a certain type of person to a specifically defined family type. Since such effects may vary according to the characteristics of other household members, MLBAM's measure of the influence of family composition on family expenditures does not strictly belong to the "Engel class" of equivalence scales. However, it is the authors' opinion that trading off these theoretical considerations yields important utilitarian value in answering applied questions regarding the effect of children on family expenditures.

COMPARISON WITH PREVIOUS STUDIES

The results in this book are the first published regional estimates of Canadian family child rearing costs by three income levels. Most previous Canadian studies have focused on establishing normative standards of what poor families should spend in order to meet the basic needs of children. Other child rearing cost studies based on examining family expenditures have been conducted primarily using data from the United States. In this section we will compare our results with two of those studies, one published by the Family Economics branch of the United States Department of Agriculture (USDA) and the second by Thomas Espenshade and the Urban Institute.

The USDA regularly publishes estimated child rearing costs for urban, rural, and farm families by level of living and region of the country in its quarterly periodical, *Family Economics Review*. USDA figures are based on U.S. family expenditure surveys, similar to Canada's Family Expenditure Survey. Although the USDA methodology has been criticized by Espenshade (1984) and others as oversimplified, USDA estimates remain the only regularly updated source of child rearing cost estimates and are in absolute dollars quite similar to those derived by other authors. For example, in 1981 the USDA (1982) estimated the cost of raising an average child at a moderate cost level to be about $75,736 while Espenshade (1984) estimated that families spent $80,000 for their second child in the same year.[5]

In 1984 Espenshade published a book using adult equivalency measures to derive child rearing costs. Although not comparable, his methodology is more consistent than the USDA methodology with that used in our study of Canadian expenditures. He estimates that families of middle socioeconomic status with a mother working part-time spend 17 to 24% of *net* income for the benefit of their first child. Our estimates indicate that Canadian families spend 10 to 14% of *gross* income to raise their first child.[6]

There are several reasons why our two estimates would differ. The first is obviously the expression of cost as a percentage of net versus gross income. If, for example, a Canadian family with a gross income of $40,000 pays 20% of income to taxes, and 10% of gross income to child rearing costs, those child rearing costs would amount to 12.5% of net income. That is, cost percentages based on gross income will be smaller than those based on net income.

A second difference between our estimates and those of both Espenshade and the USDA is that we have not included any measures of children's influence on durable good purchases such as automobiles, furniture, and recreational vehicles. Those components are included in the U.S. estimates and result in their estimates (1) being larger than ours, and (2) capturing larger economies of scale measures.

Finally, medical costs in the United States comprise a larger share of child rearing costs than in Canada where medicine is socialized. In 1987 the USDA estimated that medical costs constituted over 6% of moderate level child rearing costs over an 18-year period for families living in an urban midwestern area. Our estimates indicate that medical costs in 1982 made up about 1% of Canadian family child rearing costs.

Although there are differences in currency measures and market baskets between Canadian and American expenditures, as a simple point of comparison, in 1987 the USDA (1987) estimated that raising a child at a moderate level of living in an urban midwest area cost $95,867 (U.S.) over an 18-year period. Our child rearing cost estimates for middle-income families[7] living in British Columbia are $100,140 (Cdn.) over an 18-year period.

END NOTES

1. See Barten 1964; Blokland 1976; Buse and Salathe 1978; Espenshade 1984; Henderson 1950; Lazear and Michael 1980; Muellbauer 1980; Olson 1983; Prais and Houthakker 1955; Price, 1971; Singh and Nagar 1973; Sydenstricker and King 1921; Tedford, Capps, and Havlicek 1986; Tyrrell 1979; and Van der Gaag and Smolensky 1982.
2. See Blokland 1976; Buse and Salathe 1978; Tedford, Capps and Havlicek 1986; and Tyrrell 1979.

3. Logit models applied to decision making are most often used in cases where the dependent variable is dichotomous, involving a two alternative choices, such as the decision whether or not to attend college. The model is specified in terms of probabilities and assumes that the probability of choosing a particular alternative is distributed according to a logistic distribution function. The dependent variable in logit analysis is the probability of one alternative being selected, and is postulated to depend on several factors, such as characteristics of the alternative being selected, and attributes of the individual making the choice. Theil (1969) extended the logit model to include more than two alternatives. In terms of family expenditure allocation, we assume that 1) each share of the budget is allocated independently, 2) the probabilities of family budget allocations follow the logistic function, and 3) the assumed error structure of the model follows a Weibull distribution.
4. See also Tyrrell 1983.
5. The U.S.D.A. child rearing estimates are based on averages for all children, i.e., all children are assumed to have the same marginal cost. Espenshade estimates separate marginal effects for second and all subsequent children in order to test for the presence of economies of scale.
6. Percentages are estimated child rearing costs that include expenditures for child care and housing assuming that the family owns its own home and both parents are employed.
7. Total gross family income of $40,000 in 1988.

APPENDIX B

DETAILED DESCRIPTION OF EXPENDITURE CATEGORIES

Food at home includes all food and non-alcoholic beverages purchased from stores, including food purchased from stores while on day trips and on longer trips.

Utilities consists of spending for the family's main residence, on water, heating fuel, and electricity. Utilities which are included in the rent are classified as spending for shelter, and thus not included here. This category also includes outlays for communications, such as telephone, postal services, and other communication services.

Clothing includes outlays for infants' clothing, children's clothing and adult clothing purchased for children age 14 and older. Expenditures for outerwear, accessories, jewelry, and footwear are also part of this category.

Education and related expenditures include spending on tuition, lessons, school supplies, textbooks, and reading materials such as books and magazines, newspapers, maps, music and duplicating services, library fees and fines, and union and professional dues.

Transportation expenditures comprise spending for the operating of automobiles and trucks for personal use including fuel, maintenance and repairs, parking, driving lessons, insurance and licence fees. Additional expenditures include outlays for bus, cab, trains, plane fares, and household movers.

Health care includes money spent for eye care, eye glasses, and contact lenses, pharamaceutical products (prescribed and over-the-counter), dental care (orthodontics, etc.), and health insurance premiums.

Household operation includes outlays for household cleaning supplies, domestic help, paper, plastic and foil household supplies, horticultural goods and services, pet supplies, household and clothing textiles, services related to furnishings and clothing, hair grooming services, plus personal care supplies. Personal care supplies are composed of toilet preparations, cosmetics, oral hygiene products, soap, razors, disposable diapers, and personal care electric equipment.

Housing expenditures include rent, mortgage interest, mortgage principal, maintenance, repairs and replacements, property taxes, and homeowners insurance premiums.

Day care expenditures include day care centres and day nurseries, other child care outside the home, week-day child care in the home, and other child care in the home.

Miscellaneous includes recreation, adult goods, food away from home, adult clothing, and gifts. Recreation is composed of spending for sports and athletic equipment, playground equipment, toys, games and hobby equipment, photographic goods and services, musical instruments and accessories, collectors' items (excluding works of art), camping and picnic equipment (except barbecues), recreational vehicles and outboard motors, bicycles, operation of recreational vehicles, home-entertainment equipment and services, use of recreational facilities, travel tours, spectator-entertainment performances such as movies, plays, and live sports, and other recreation services. Adult goods include spending for alcoholic beverages, both purchased from stores and served on licensed premises, tobacco products and smokers' supplies, and lottery and raffle tickets. Food away from home is food purchased from restaurants and fast-food establishments. Gifts include payments for spousal and child support, money gifts to charitable organizations, and gifts to people not in the immediate family. Also included in miscellaneous are legal expenses, spending on financial services, tools and equipment purchased for work, fines, passports, and funeral services.

APPENDIX C

INCOME GROWTH AND DISCOUNT FACTORS

TABLE C1

REAL INCOME GROWTH FACTORS AT 2% (COMPOUNDED) PER YEAR

Year	Factor
1	1.02
2	1.04
3	1.06
4	1.08
5	1.10
6	1.13
7	1.15
8	1.17
9	1.20
10	1.22
11	1.24
12	1.27
13	1.29
14	1.32
15	1.35
16	1.37
17	1.40
18	1.43
19	1.46
20	1.49
21	1.52
22	1.55
23	1.58
24	1.61
25	1.64

Table C2

Discount Factors at Discount Rates from 1-5%

Year	Discount rate				
	1%	2%	3%	4%	5%
1	.990	.980	.971	.962	.952
2	.980	.961	.943	.925	.907
3	.971	.942	.915	.889	.864
4	.961	.924	.888	.855	.823
5	.951	.906	.862	.822	.784
6	.942	.888	.837	.790	.746
7	.933	.871	.813	.760	.711
8	.923	.853	.789	.731	.677
9	.914	.837	.766	.703	.645
10	.905	.820	.744	.676	.614
11	.896	.804	.722	.650	.585
12	.887	.788	.701	.623	.557
13	.879	.773	.681	.601	.530
14	.870	.758	.661	.577	.505
15	.861	.743	.641	.555	.481
16	.853	.728	.623	.534	.458
17	.844	.714	.605	.513	.436
18	.836	.700	.587	.494	.416
19	.828	.686	.570	.475	.396
20	.820	.673	.554	.456	.377
21	.811	.660	.538	.439	.359
22	.803	.646	.523	.422	.342
23	.795	.634	.507	.406	.323
24	.788	.622	.492	.390	.310
25	.780	.610	.478	.375	.295

REFERENCES

Almon, S.
  1965   "The distributed lag between capital appropriations and expenditures." *Econometrica* 33: 178-96.
Barten, A.P.
  1964   "Family composition, prices and expenditure patterns", pp 227-92. in P.E. Hart, G. Mills and J.K. Whitaker (eds.), *Econometric analysis for national economic planning*. London: Butterworths.
Blokland, J.
  1976   *Continuous consumer equivalence scales*. Leiden: Stenfert Kroese.
Buse, R. and Salathe, L.
  1978   Adult equivalent scales: An alternative approach. *American Journal of Agricultural Economics* 60: 460-68.
Douthitt, R.A. and Fedyk, J.M.
  1988   "The influence of children on family life-cycle spending behavior: Theory and applications." *Journal of Consumer Affairs* 22: 220-48.
Engel, E.
  1895   "Die Lebenskosten Belgischer Arbeiter-Familien fruher and jetzt." *International Statistical Institute Bulletin* 9: 1-74.
Espenshade, T.J.
  1984   *Investing in children*. Washington, D.C.: The Urban Institute.
Forsyth, F.G.
  1960   "The relationship between family size and family expenditure." *Royal Statistical Society Journal* 123: 367-93.
Friedman, M.
  1957   *A theory of the consumption function*. Princeton: Princeton University Press.
Henderson, A.M.
  1950   "The cost of children. Parts II and III." *Population Studies* 4: 267-98.
Lazear, F.P. and Michael, R.T.
  1980   "Family size and the distribution of real per capita income". *American Economic Review* 70: 91-107.
Muellbauer, J.
  1980   "The estimation of the Prais-Houthakker model of equivalence scales". *Econometrica* 48: 153-76.
Olson, L.
  1983   *Costs of children*. Toronto: Lexington Books.
Prais, S.J. and Houthakker, H.S.
  1955   *The analysis of family budgets*. Cambridge: Cambridge University Press.
Price, D.W.
  1971   Unit equivalence scales for specific food commodities. *American Journal of Agricultural Economics* 52: 224-33.

Singh, B. and Nagar, A.L.
      1973   Determination of consumer unit scales". *Econometrica* 41: 347-55.
Sydenstricker, F. and King, W.I.
      1921   "The measurement of the relative economic status of families".
              Quarterly Publication of the American Statistical Association 17: 842-57.
Tedford, J.R., Capps, O. and Havlicek, J.
      1986   "Adult equivalence scales once more — a developmental
              approach". *American Journal of Agricultural Economics* 68(2): 321-33.
Theil, H.
      1969   "A multinomial extension of the linear logit model". *International
              Economic Review* 10: 251-58.
Tyrell, T.J.
      1983   "The use of polynomials to shift coefficients in linear regression
              models". *Journal of Business and Economic Statistics* 1:249-52.
      1979.   *An application of the multinomial logit model to predicting the pattern of
              food and other household expenditures in the northeastern United States.*
              Dissertation, Cornell University.
U.S. Department of Agriculture.
      1987   "Updated estimates of the cost of raising a child." *Family Economics
              Review* (Winter), 36-37.
U.S. Department of Agriculture.
      1982   "Updated estimates of the cost of raising a child." *Family Economics
              Review* (Winter), 30-31.
Van der Gaag, J. and Smolensky, E.
      1982   "True household equivalence scales and characteristics of the poor
              in the United States." *Review of Income and Wealth* 28: 17-28.